First, Let's Kill the Lawyer Jokes

An Attorney's Irreverent
Serious Look at the
Legal Universe

MARCEL STRIGBERGER

PRAISE FOR MARCEL STRIGBERGER
FOR *BIRTH, DEATH AND OTHER TRIVIALITIES*

"Marcel Strigberger is an irrepressible humorist with a story teller's flair for spinning a yarn with true (and hysterically funny) insights into the basics of human nature."

—*Midwest Book Review*

"Marcel Strigberger has produced an often-amusing collection of short reflections of such topics as health and happiness, religion and, of course, the law."

—*The Globe and Mail*

"This quickly paced book makes it entertaining and intriguing to contemplate life."

—*Matrimonial Affairs* (Canadian Bar Association, Family Law Section)

FOR *POUTINE ON THE ORIENT EXPRESS*

"Get ready for a joyous journey filled with Marcel's wit + wisdom. You will be traveling many delightful miles with Marcel as your tour guide as he provides enlightening commentary with just the right light touch. When Marcel takes you along for the ride, you'll see that his mirth is universal—whether you spell it "humour" or "humor.""

—Dr. Joel Goodman
Founder/Director of The HUMOR Project, Inc.

"Marcel Strigberger's entertaining book brings thoughtful, insightful, twisted, and funny views to the travel experience. And from my personal point of view, that's what good humour is all about. Keep laughing!"

—Dave Schwensen, author of *How to Be a Working Comic*
Former talent coordinator for A&E's *An Evening at the Improv*

"There are lots of books about travel, and lots of funny books, but not many funny books about travel. In this book Toronto wit Strigberger is working at the top of his game."

—Mark Breslin, CEO and founder of Yuks Yuks

FOR *BOOMERS, ZOOMERS, AND OTHER OOMERS*

"This book is fantastic! I didn't stop reading it until the end. It's witty, insightful and engaging. It speaks to multiple generations."

—Jeremy Miller, author of *Sticky Branding*

"Marcel touches on the topic of aging with both humour and grace. He reminds us that if we can't laugh at ourselves at THIS age, we're definitely taking life too seriously. And really, age only matters if you're a grape. In which case, you're really wine. We all get better with age."

—Mona Andrei, author of *Superwoman: A Funny and Reflective Look at Single Motherhood*

"In reading Marcel's book, I felt like I was taking an enjoyable walk down memory lane with a knowledgeable guide. Most important, I got some great laughs too."

—Dr. Riley E. Moynes, author of *The Four Phases of Retirement*

"In our wisdom years we possess the ability and the luxury to see life through humour. Your book fulfills a real need."

—Dr. Zvi Lanir, author of *The Wisdom Years*

FOR *FIRST, LET'S KILL THE LAWYER JOKES*

Marcel Strigberger's new book about lawyers is a well-written and entertaining account of the legal profession that will amuse and inform anyone who reads it. Drawing effectively on his rich experience as a practising lawyer, Strigberger mixes insight, wisdom (and practical advice), with a large helping of irreverent humour.

Philip Slayton, author of *Lawyers Gone Bad*

Marcel is a judicial Aristotle, with a healthy dose of wit and humour. This book is an uplifting read for all, lawyers and other mortals.

Eugene Meehan, K.C., Supreme Advocacy, Ottawa

An inspiring, honest, witty appraisal of the legal system by an insightful raconteur with a trademark sense of humour. A must read!

The Honourable Sandra Chapnik, former judge and author of *Bold Decisions: Memoirs of a Judge, Lawyer, Teacher and Working Mom*

How many lawyers does it take to write an insightful, hilarious look at the legal industry from inside and out and then publish those musings in a collection of bite-sized reads that takes readers into courtrooms around the world and rivals for fun and efficiency that other literary classic *Uncle John's Bathroom Reader*? One! And he is Marcel Strigberger, the most prolific legal funny guy in the universe.

What's it like working with Strigberger? Imagine having Dave Barry as your lawyer. That's all you have to know.

Now go buy Strigberger's *First, Let's Kill the Lawyer Jokes: An Attorney's Irreverent Serious Look at the Legal Universe*.

—Peter Carter, Analysis Editor, Law 360

FOR *HUMOUR (HUMOR?) TALENTS GENERALLY*

"Strigberger is a comically gifted lawyer."

—*The Lawyers Weekly*

"Strigberger presents his material in his witty, stand-up comedy style."

—*Lifestyles*

"Strigberger's personality jumps off the page, with his humble humor and sharp wit."

—Blair Chavis, Assistant Managing Editor at the *ABA Journal*

Bless you all!

—Marcel Strigberger

First, Let's Kill the Lawyer Jokes
An Attorney's Irreverent Serious Look at the Legal Universe
Marcel Strigberger

THREE BEANS
PRESS

Marcelshumour.com

ISBN: 978-0-9959501-4-6 (print)
ISBN: 978-0-9959501-5-3 (ePub)

CONTENTS

ACKNOWLEDGEMENTS

Did you ever wonder whether writing a book can get lonely? It can and it does. I can take great comfort that I had a number of kind and competent people I was able to bother when I got tired talking to myself. This is as good a time and place as any to acknowledge some of these gracious souls.

Let me start with my editor, Andrea Lemieux. I was of the illusion for ages that we are all editors in that all it takes to get it right is to run the Word spell check. Illusion shattered. Andrea recrafted my manuscript knowing when to distinguish "could" from "can," "that" from "which," and numbering, such as "seven" from "7."

She also ably fact checked my comments along the way, noting errors I made such as thinking that Starbuck's large coffee size was called "Grande." What can possibly leave anybody to come to that conclusion otherwise?

Most encouraging, Andrea told me that reading my manuscript often made her laugh out loud. I don't know. If an editor laughs out loud in the forest, does she make a sound? The mystery remains. Thanx Andrea.

I also wish to thank and acknowledge people who were good enough to spend time reading my drafts or listening to my pleas, and who otherwise gave me sage and priceless feedback, much of which I followed.

Thank you, Eugene Meehan, K.C., who authors his weekly informative newsletter, *Supreme Advocacy*, and who is the guru of persuasive legal writing. He notes that lawyers are at their best when they don't sound like lawyers. I have taken his advice seriously, and for starters, ensured the book does not contain any Latin words. OK, minimis.

And thanx to The Honourable Sandra Chapnik, former judge, and author of *Bold Decisions: Memoirs of a Judge, Lawyer, Teacher, and Working Mom*. A great read proving that contrary to what some of us think, judges are human.

I much appreciate the praise and encouragement of double colleague Michael Cochrane, lawyer and best-selling author of fiction and non-fiction. Being Canadian, make that double double.

I also am grateful to Philip Slayton, lawyer, former professor, and author of several books including bestseller *Lawyers Gone Bad*. The stories about how some of these lawyers landed in jail are fascinating. Philip was actually my prof at McGill over fifty years ago. He even told me back then, "Marcel, how about we touch base once your book is done—in about fifty years." Actually, he did not remember me but he's still the inspirational eclectic guy he was back then.

All these great books are available on Amazon, and at other fine retailers.

Hey Peter Carter, Analysis Editor, *Law 360*, who kept me busy and in shape honing my craft by giving me the opportunity to pen a weekly column to lighten up the lives of lawyers, who, like the rest of us these times, can use some lightening up. This man has a super sense of humour, the second funniest guy in the country.

Finally, I want to thank my wife, Shoshana, and kids, Daniel, Natalie, and Gabriel, and their respective offspring, for their support in not suggesting that I am in any way retired. They have also been helpful in assisting me with tech matters, such as translating into English my discussions with associates at the Apple store.

Finally, one more, or as Columbo would say, "Just one more thing madame." Thanx to Abraham Lincoln, Albert Einstein, Yogi Berra, and others for your great comments, which I have graciously quoted throughout this opus.

And of course, thank you all, dear readers. We all crave good humour (ok, humor to our neighbours to the south). Thanx for showing up. You good. We are now all on the same page.

Cheers.

INTRODUCTION

Hi everybody. Welcome to this unique, exclusive, and definitely one-of-a-kind tour of the legal universe. My stories are based on over forty years of practising civil and criminal law in the Toronto area. I come here not to praise lawyers but to bury misconceptions.

There are no lawyer jokes here. I have disposed of the lawyer jokes. Actually, there is one. Here it is: Lawyers don't think they're funny and non-lawyers don't think they're jokes.

Done.

A question you might be asking yourself: Do I need to be a lawyer to understand this book? Not at all. Lawyers may identify more with some of the content but non-lawyers will not only get it but they will also laugh more. Guaranteed. You see, lawyers are often afraid to express their sense of humour for fear of not being taken seriously. More about this handicap later on.

You will not come across too many nine-dollar legal words such as whereases, hereinbefores, and hereafters, and definitely no Latin lingo. Promise. Not one word. Zero. Nada. Nihil. I am deeming all Latin words and phrases ultra *vires* (i.e., beyond the boundaries, over the top, a no no).

You will read stories about what lay people think about judges, why the public loves lawyers (it's not all non-fiction), and why many lawyers are not happy about their choice of law as a career to the extent that some might even consider applying for a job as a driver of an Oscar Meyer Wienermobile.

We'll explore the courtroom, including its characters in addition to lawyers, such as witnesses, judges, juries, and that mystery old man who just sits there and does nothing.

To assist non-lawyers and non-legal folks to best understand this book, I thought it a good idea to include a brief glossary of legal terms. You may not be familiar with these esoteric, cryptic, mystical terms:

1. The Judge

He or she is the king or queen of the courtroom. They can make life-altering decisions from whether you go to prison to getting a large sum of money. You can recognize them as they usually sit on a high bench dressed in a flourishing robe; they often scowl at you. They used to be lawyers before getting appointed to the bench, but they often forget what it was like to be a lawyer in a pressure-cooker practice. Many suffer from what is known as "judgitis." You don't want to get them angry. Then again, many are just fine. I say this as it is the truth. As well, though I am retired from practice, I may one day find myself before one in a courtroom and I don't want to general-ize for fear of provoking their wrath. And believe me, they can be wrathful. More about judges and other characters to follow in chapter nineteen.

2. The jury

This is a group of six or twelve people who, although they generally have no idea of legal matters but by virtue of some English law going back to 1215 known as the *Magna Carta* (did I just use a Latin word?—Oops! Excuse please. My bad. *Mea culpa*). They also get to decide on little matters such as whether you go to prison or whether you get a large sum of money (or don't). They generally get dragged, kicking and screaming, into duty for little or no money. You know they're in a good mood. You don't want to get under their skin either. More to follow in chapter nineteen.

3. The witness

They can often help your case. They come to the courtroom and swear and are expected to tell the truth. Then again, the Toronto Maple Leafs play hockey and though they have not done so since 1967, this season they expect to win the Stanley Cup.

4. The little old man who just sits in the courtroom and does nothing
I'll have more to say about him too in chapter nineteen. Please do not jump there now. I know you're curious. He'll wait for you.

5. The lawyers
Are you kidding? Everybody knows what lawyers are. We're generally OK.

I was called to the Bar of Ontario in 1974 B.C. (before computers). I will confess now that I am an old-school baby boomer technophobe. For some reason I was never at ease with technology. I experienced typewriters, dial phones, carbon copies, and live people answering the phone. I know you millennials ask, what is a live person? Got it.

So, fasten your seatbelts. What better way to start than by looking at the history of lawyers.

CHAPTER ONE

History of Lawyers—non-Biased

"It's like déjà vu all over again"
~ Yogi Berra

I ask, where in history do we see lawyers mentioned? Actually, after thinking about it I see no sign of lawyers for millennia. Let's start in the beginning. The good Lord forbids Adam and Eve from eating from the tree of knowledge. They disobey and there is trouble. You might say all hell breaks loose in the Garden of Eden. They have to go fig leaf. Then they get booted out of this ideal residence.

Would it have helped if they had a lawyer to plead their case? As a lawyer, I say "of course." However, since Adam blamed Eve for hounding him, you would have needed two lawyers: obvious conflict of interest. Make that three lawyers—let's not forget that talking serpent. Three lawyers for two humans and one snake. No wonder the world eventually saw a glut of lawyers. But not yet.

Forward onto Cain and Abel—history's first homicide. When confronted by God as to Abel's whereabouts, Cain blurts out, "Am I my brother's keeper?" This would have been an opportune time to have a lawyer argue for Cain's right to remain silent. But alas, no lawyer. Cain may not have had much of a legal defence. What could he say? "My brother Abel made these sacrifices on the alter and they were accepted. My offerings went nowhere. What I did was self-defence." Nonetheless a lawyer could have made a pitch as to sentence. "Your Honour, my client is a first offender. He has no criminal record. We ask that you not put any marks on his forehead." Who knows what the result would have been had Cain had legal representation.

Jumping ahead a few begats to Noah. Even if there were lawyers, Noah certainly did not invite them aboard the ark. Why not? Maybe he retained one to advise him on say, environmental issues. But there was a dispute about the bill so he decided to throw his lawyer under the bus, or rather, under the ark. I suppose had he had one aboard, this would have represented history's first in-house counsel.

Centuries later Moses comes down the mountain lugging two stone tablets bearing the Ten Commandments. Not being a spring chicken, chances are he would have injured himself. I'm much younger and I have problems dragging out the trash. Perhaps he did hurt his back but there was no lawyer around to advise him of his workers' compensation rights. The book of Exodus is definitely silent on this issue. I checked. Just stuff about a sea splitting, some golden calf idol worship, and a plague or two (not sure which variants; Greek letters were not around yet).

Speaking of ancient Greece, we see orators like Demosthenes doing the talking for others. Demo was a great speaker, practising talking with pebbles in his mouth. (Caution colleagues: Do not try this one at home.) But orators were not lawyers *per se*. I have seen no evidence of archeologists coming across a shingle reading something like, "Demosthenes: If I don't win, you don't pay."

We start seeing some semblance to the legal profession in ancient Rome. However, for ages these advocates were prohibited from charging a fee. Eventually Emperor Claudius fixed this problem somewhat, but permissible fees had a low ceiling of 10,000 sestertii. I am not sure what this amounts to as all I could find was that 4 sestertii equalled one denarius.

However, lawyers were complaining that they could not make a decent living. Regardless of what work they did, after a while they had to stop the meter from running. Presumably this remuneration status likely led to the phrase *pro bono*. Who knows? It certainly wasn't *bono* for the lawyers.

Then for the next millennium plus, we hear diddly about lawyers. I googled "Dark Ages any lawyers, hello?" I found nothing even remotely resembling anything like "Goth, Visigoth, and Leif the Lucky Barristers and Solicitors."

And I wonder if a lawyer drafted the *Magna Carta*. I'd say this would garner some awesome testimonials on his website. "We retained Norman to draft the *Magna Carta*. He finished it in a timely manner and at a reasonable cost. We would definitely use his services again." Maybe it was drafted by a lawyer, or by some paralegal called Egbert. That sounds like a good name for a thirteenth-century paralegal. Your guess is as good as mine.

Interestingly, I note Chaucer's *Canterbury Tales* does not include a lawyer. Of numerous callings, nowhere is there a "Lawyer's Tale." Why? Maybe the pilgrims did not want one along the pilgrimage.

Perhaps Chaucer initially had a lawyer in there but canned him. There just may have been a draft tale that reads like, "And then there was the lawyer from Yorke who carried a big purse. And he was a windbagge. He tried to impress us with his Latin and we couldn't understand him, and so the miller gave him a big kick in the arse. And we were all happy, *Pater Noster*.

Actually, Chaucer does mention a "Man of Law," but it is not clear whether or not this gentleman was a lawyer. Maybe he was but the other pilgrims did not take too kindly to him. Maybe they all had something to fear or dislike about lawyers. The Physician may have asserted, "Drop him lest he sues me for malpractice." Or the Wife of Bath may have commented, "My lawyer cleaned me out during my divorce case. I really took a bath." Or the Monk simply said, "No lawyers here. They talk too much." If it's any consolation, this eclectic group did not include a dentist either. No clue why.

The next reference to lawyers that I could think of did not make me too comfortable. I speak of Shakespeare's reference, "The first thing we do, let's kill all the lawyers." Provocative comments such as this might certainly discourage some law-school prospects from writing the LSATs. (The LSAT is an aptitude test wanna-be law students have to write before applying to law school. Sort of an IQ test for lawyers.)

At least not mentioning lawyers is preferable to threatening them. Better silence. Like that monk.

Charles Dickens is kinder with his Sidney Carton lawyer character in *A Tale of Two Cities*. This English barrister gentleman switches places with a French-look doppelgänger, choosing to take his place with Madame Guillotine. I'd say portrayal of this character was a far, far better thing that happened to lawyers' reputations than anything most authors have done.

Personally, I first heard of lawyers as a grade schooler watching *Perry Mason*. Episode after episode Mason would get clients off the hook who were charged with murder.

I do recall that Perry Mason did not discuss fees too often with his clients. His able assistant, Della Street, would just say over the intercom, "There's a Mr. Ferguson in the waiting room who was just accused of the fatal stabbing of real-estate magnate, Miles Lashley. He wants to retain you but says he has no money. Mason would respond, "I'll take the case. Send him in."

I guess there is more to happiness than a few *sestertii*. More about Perry Mason later.

In grade school I was the class comedian, and for my efforts my teacher, Mr. Webster, used to inflict cruel and unusual punishment. He would make me write out twenty times, "I shall not joke in class." I thought to myself, where is the justice? I so much wanted to call out Mr. Webster and other Mr. Websters. But at that time I was not even aware of the concept of a lawyer. I have no clue how the world functioned without lawyers for millennia. After all we are the gatekeepers of access to justice. I do know I am proud of our noble profession. I don't really care what others thought about us, like that physician, Wife of Bath, or that monk.

CHAPTER TWO

Why Everybody Loves Lawyers—Sort Of

"To me, a lawyer is basically the person that knows the rules of
the country. We're all throwing the dice, playing the game, moving our pieces around the board, but if there's a problem, the lawyer
is the only person that has read the inside of the top of the box."
~ Jerry Seinfeld

Now that we have concluded that the legal profession is relatively a
young one, let's explore what the public thinks about lawyers.
Unfortunately, lay people often view us negatively as sharks, shysters, and
ambulance chasers.

We face a barrage of unflattering lawyer jokes. As noted, only one
lawyer joke per book. We shall not be repeating this barrage.

A poll conducted a couple of years ago by the Ontario Bar Association
found that only 44% of the public trusted lawyers. We lawyers scored less
trust than plumbers. And we just beat out auto mechanics and taxi drivers. Phew!

I get the feeling it would not be a great idea for a lawyer's website to read, "See us about your divorce. While you wait, let us do your oil change. We also give you the best deals to the airport."

So, the question becomes, why is our profession generally viewed unsympathetically?

My thoughts.

Dollars

We are talking hundreds per hour. I have heard more than once colleagues saying something like, "if I ever get divorced, I couldn't afford myself." (Never mind the part about if they would hire themselves, they'd have a fool for a client.) Then again lawyers are not the highest paid individuals. Corporate executives, many physicians, and certainly athletes earn more. I note soccer star Lionel Messi earns over $100 million per year, almost half of which is from endorsements. Other athletes also earn in the millions. Yet I don't hear anybody saying, "This guy gets two million dollars just for saying something like, 'I wear Adidas sneakers. They're cool. Yo.'"

The Toronto Maple Leafs players earn many times over per player than the average lawyer. They have not won a Stanley cup in almost half a century and have not advanced past the second round in the playoffs in years.

Do we ever hear a survey that concludes that the public does not trust hockey players? How many people do you know who would rather watch plumbers at work?

We already do some *pro bono* or free work here and there (though not always voluntarily), more than most professional athletes who get paid much more than most lawyers, even when they lose.

Honesty and Transparency

Most lawyers are above board, straight as an arrow, telling it as it is. But what does the public see, or not see? We live in the Uber age. If you want to go from A to B, Uber will instantly confirm up front the exact cost, such as $13.43. And the customer can verify this service, seeing he is not going from A to C.

We can understand why a client will get rattled when he sees his lawyer's bill for thousands—and he has not even gone to court yet. Actually, lawyers do spend time out of court communicating with people; drafting document briefs; and preparing for meetings, examinations, and court. A fisherman has to spend time working on his boat and nets before he goes out to sea. It's not like the fish just swim out to shore and shout, "Where do you want us to stand."

Then again, I suppose the customer will say something like, "All I care about is the size and quality of that tuna. I'm not buying the net."

I shall have more to say about legal fees when I discuss billing. Save the worst for later. I won't talk about those lawyers who strayed and are now in jail (or as Chaucer would say, "in *gaol*, and *goode* for them").

Ambulance Chasers

There is no shortage of lawyers. But the public must find disturbing those ubiquitous ads. I shall not quote any names but suffice it to say they do not come across anything like, "We try harder." (Actually, after fifty years Avis changed its tagline to "It's your space.")

Many ads cross the line. There is actually a local firm that posts its ads on the walls over urinals. This adds a new dimension to the phrase, "over the top."

I just returned from a trip in Florida. What caught my eye most is not the great weather, nor the kilometres of super beaches, nor the cultural scenes. What really hit me was lawyer advertising. You cannot turn on your television or walk around the block without getting slapped by yet another personal-injury lawyer ad. In fact, you don't even have to turn on your television to get smitten by these ads. When I checked into my hotel room, I opened my night-table drawer and I noticed a yellow-pages directory. On the front cover there was an ad that listed a law firm's name and info, including "Injured in an accident? Call us first. You can check out the Gideon Bible later."

They even have easy-to-remember phone numbers. You will see some that read like, 1-800-111-1111. In our jurisdiction that number will more likely get you a pizza. I even saw one that read something like, "Injured? Just call 1-800-not-pain." I am sure some in-your-face high-profile outfit that is rougher than the roughest will soon come up with the ultimate contact: "Injured? Call any phone number. You will reach us."

I even saw a bus, or rather a number of municipal buses, in Fort Lauderdale bearing a full side of the bus ad for a personal-injury firm. These lawyers take hunting for accident files to a new dimension. They use buses to chase ambulances! And many of them boast about having offices throughout Florida. Just call us. I expect them to expand their ad soon to say, "If there is no office near where you live, we'll open one for you."

And then they have the sub-specialists. While driving on the highway I-95 I saw a billboard that read, "Motorcycle accident? Call the lawyer who rides a Harley." Another ad reads, "Chosen by *Super Lawyers Magazine*." I have heard of great lawyers but what in the world is a super lawyer? He changes into his suit in a phone booth?

The phone-book ads appear not under "lawyers" but rather under "attorneys." After gazing through these ads for a few minutes, I needed a break and so I flipped back a few pages and just before attorneys I came across "asphalt." I saw an ad for a "Dr Asphalt." This was rather refreshing. At least he did not boast, "as seen on TV," "want a second opinion," or "chosen by *Super Asphalt Magazine*."

Talk Too Much

Lawyers are generally perceived as being long-winded. I wanted to connect to a Starbucks Wi-Fi recently. I had to run a gauntlet of conditions, spending fifteen minutes doing so. Meanwhile, my cappuccino cooled off. (I will confess I also had the inexplicable urge after reading the document to bill someone.)

Most lay people likely simply click "agree," griping about those overpaid lawyers making life complicated.

I opened the link and I believe I am probably the only person who ever read this stuff, other than maybe the lawyer who drafted it after graduating from Attila the Hun Law School. Draconian? You decide. They go something like this:

Privacy?

• Ha, ha, ha! We have the right to share all your user information with necessary third parties. Necessary third parties include Starbucks, Google, and Amazon. As well, your personal information may find itself on Mark Zuckerberg's Facebook page. If you see it there, you hereby agree to like it.

• We have the right to install cookies of our choice on your device. Today we are installing blueberry scones.

Improper Use of Wi-Fi

• You agree not to use your device for any improper purposes, including spam, copyright infringement, or defamatory postings. If you burn yourself on the hot coffee or tea, you agree to limit your reactions to saying "ouch."

• You may not transmit viruses, worms, or Trojan horses. You will be required to clean up any mess made by any such horses.

Offensive Language

• You will not use offensive terms, phrases, or language, including Canadian. These include but are not limited to the Canadian words "Timbits," "double-double," or "zed."

Damages

• You use this service at your own risk. We are not responsible for damages, injuries, or traumas, however caused, other than those governed by the 2013 Sumatran Java Convention. In such case, damages will be limited to one venti cappuccino (275 calories). For strawberry or vanilla extract please add fifty cents.

As the old adage says, "There is no such thing as a free latte." Is there anybody who does not agree? Click here.

And not only do lawyers talk too much, but the public also faults them for the way they communicate, using all these Latin words and phrases.

Why are lawyers more mistrusted? Maybe it is also the way we communicate. Unlike hockey players, we have our own language, legalese. Perhaps this annoys the lay people. We use terms like "examination for discovery," "pleadings," and those dreaded Latin words and phrases such as *Factum, res ipse loquitor*, and *habeus corpus*. The public probably believes we charge more for using these words. Maybe they have a point. After all, I have never heard the Great one, Wayne Gretsky, interviewed, and he talked about taking a swing with his "stickum" and slapping the "puckum" into the "netta." And when he got a hat trick, I never heard him say he scored three "goali."

Perhaps lawyers can learn something from the athletes. Win or lose, keep it simple. Don't try to show off. I'll have more to say about communication.

Duration of Case

Most cases linger, often taking years to resolve. This is certainly on the opposite end of the spectrum compared to the duration of services rendered by the workers of the world's oldest profession. And presumably the latter's services are more pleasurable.

Why does a legal case, and I am talking litigation, take so long to resolve? For example, a dentist's work, say, is generally done within an hour—fortunately! A doctor's examination can be measured in minutes. Even surgery will take only hours.

Yet resolution of a personal-injury case will not happen for several years. As an accident is generally a novel experience for most people, they are not aware of the dynamics of a personal injury claim, consisting of investigation, marshalling medical evidence, waiting for the injuries to crystallize, and of course following the procedural steps of examinations under oath, mediation, and ultimately in some cases a trial. And given that in personal-injury cases the lawyer does not even get paid until there is a resolution, I would expect the client to view the lawyer as also being a victim. But alas the client does not see it this way. Fair enough. All is forgiven.

The best we can do about this issue is to clearly explain the process to the clients, reassuring them that the reason for the delay is not their lawyer spending too much time golfing. Or maybe playing soccer.

Unsavoury Clients
The public does not like it when we represent notorious criminals. A most common comment I get is, "How can you represent someone you just know is guilty?"

Bearing this in mind, to improve our image, maybe the criminal lawyer should respond, "You have a point madam, I am going to the jail this afternoon and I shall advise my client to plead guilty." The lawyer should be careful not to add, "How about that oil change?"

The Law Itself
Often a client has a great case but for the fact that given the passage of time, it is statute barred. The public does not know that generally you have ten days to notify a municipality if you slip on a sidewalk, or six months to sue the government for a tort or accident, as in the latter in Canada, you are suing the King and he, or Rex, gets special protection. Nor do most people know that an accused has the right not to testify, and the judge cannot tell a jury that there is a good reason why he is not taking the stand, like he's probably guilty and he does not want to risk confirming it. Of course, these weird laws are made by those athletic lawyers.

What can lawyers do? It would help to bill reasonably and transparently. Our ads should not look as though they were commissioned by the

Ringling brothers. And we should bend over backwards to communicate adequately with humility and simplicity. In other words, lawyers should not sound like lawyers. I rest my case. For now.

CHAPTER THREE

Communication:
Do Lawyers Get It Right?
Yes and No

"If you can't explain it to a six-year-old, you don't
understand it well enough yourself."
~ Albert Einstein

This is as good a time as any to talk about communication. Do we sometimes get it wrong? We lawyers have Errors and Omission Insurance coverage in the event we screw up. Studies have shown that a prime reason for messing up was not so much that the lawyer did not know the law, but more so that there was miscommunication between the lawyer and the client. Get it?

I learned a valuable lesson while still an articling student. At a lunch with my mentor Hank, I ordered a tea. As I like it a certain strength, I said to the waiter, one Jean Pierre, "Bag out please." He returned, and after putting the teapot and cup down he gingerly removed the hot teabag from the teapot. I reminded him that I asked for the bag out. He seemed surprised, exclaiming the bag was out. Hank smiled like the Cheshire Cat. He said,

"You just learned a basic lesson in communicating. Be as specific as possible. We are all wired differently. As long as this human condition persists, lawyers will be kept busy."

I thought about the aforementioned sage Albert Einstein, i.e., that part about, "If you can't explain it to a six-year-old, you don't understand it well enough yourself."

I believed I understood exactly how I wanted my tea. I wanted to dip the teabag myself. But I did not say that. This little incident raised my articulation antennae going forward.

I had a motor vehicle case once where my client referred me to a key witness, Roger. Roger was one of my client's close pub friends. I asked Roger whether he had consumed any alcohol prior to the accident. He replied, "Oh yeah. I had a few straight shots of scotch." After slapping my forehead, I called my client to report this possible hurdle. The client insisted Roger's drinking interlude occurred after the accident. Confused, I called Roger again, and lo and behold he thought the word "prior" meant after. Live and learn. Presumably Roger was never an active participant in contributing to the Wikipedia dictionary.

We lawyers often overwhelm our clients with lawyer talk. I once was responding to a motion to dismiss my client's action by summary judgement, i.e., before trial. My client, Vlad, was a hard-nosed construction worker and he expected kick-ass no-nonsense service. Vlad originated from Eastern Europe and his English was OK, but you had to take care not to overuse lawyerly language, otherwise you would lose him.

We met together with Harold, a newly called lawyer assisting me. Harold started explaining the motion to Vlad, but without reading our client at all. His discourse went something like, "Routinely a legal dispute results in a trier of fact determining the merits of the claim on *viva voce* evidence. However, pursuant to Rule 21, subsections 1 to 3(c) of the Consolidated Rules of Practice and Procedure, a party may launch a motion for a final order dispensing with a hearing of witnesses in persona and to have the cause of action adjudicated upon via a summary ruling based on documentary argument ..."

Vlad rolled his eyes and snapped impatiently at Harold, "Enough! Quiet! You talk too much, like voman." At that point I got a great flash of an idea. I thought it might be wise for me to take over the briefing. I asked Harold to let me continue and meanwhile to get us some tea. (At least he already knew how I liked my tea.)

I subsequently had a talk with Harold. I'm not confident he understood the lesson as a few days later he asked a client whether she owned her house in "fee simple." (Meaning highest form of ownership, outright, absolutely, i.e., all hers. I guess not one of these adjectives satisfied lawyer Harold.)

During my years of practice, I was always determined to make sure that what was being said was understood. I would always use the simplest words, especially with clients, saying instead of "lessor," "landlord;" instead of "affidavit," "sworn document;" and instead of asking for a retainer, I asked for some money. Clients understood that. And I never used the term *pro bono*. I did not want to chance giving the clients exaggerated ideas about my generosity.

Some words suggesting understanding may seem helpful but aren't, such as "you know," as in, "you must always tell the truth you know." "Oh really? I didn't know that." Nor do we here as Canadians have a unique comprehension silver bullet with the word, "eh."

Lawyer: You understand this forty-page separation agreement?

Client: "Not exactly."

Lawyer (Canadian version): "You understand this forty-page separation agreement, eh?"

Client: "Ahhh, of course. Crystal clear."

I would always repeat the gist of my discussions and ask if they were understood. One client, a former army colonel, responded with an interesting phrase, "copy that." He explained that it is used in the military to signify that the discussion is understood. I started using it too, but I soon dropped it as too often I had to explain to my puzzled listeners what it meant. They rarely copied that.

A phrase I often heard to my delight was "I got it." Sometimes clients would use an elevated version, namely "I totally got it." I was satisfied with either version.

The colonel also explained another expression for acknowledging understanding, and this was "Roger." I did use this one more often given my positive association of the word with that witness I mentioned, "prior."

We lawyers often shove documents in front of our clients asking them to sign them. I never used those stickie strips saying "sign here." I felt it put undue pressure on the clients. The stickies may as well read, "I'm Don Corleone. If you know what's good for you, sign."

I will add that Harold used to call clients in to "Execute" documents. However, whatever I said about Harold, I will say he taught me an important lesson. And that is how not to communicate.

As lawyers we must be careful with our words. I actually tested Hank's lesson by returning to that restaurant and saying to Jean Pierre, "One tea please. Just put the bag on the side; I'll dip it myself." It worked.

CHAPTER FOUR

Do We Lawyers Unnecessarily Complicate Simple Matters? Yes and No—Maybe?

"A lawyer is a person who writes a 10,000-
word document and calls it a "brief."
~ Franz Kafka

D o we lawyers unnecessarily complicate matters? Are we windbags? Do we waste too much time on trivialities? I am thinking about a comment reputedly made by the notable nineteenth-century British judge, Lord Bacon V-C, who said after a hearing: "This case bristles with simplicity. The facts are admitted, the law is plain, and yet it has taken seven days to try—one day longer than God Almighty required to make the world."

Actually, I could not readily locate the name of this case. I spent about ten minutes trying to find it but no luck. (OK, maybe twenty minutes.)

Is this problem always the fault of the lawyers? Our *Rules of Professional Conduct* note that, "advocates must raise fearlessly every issue, advance every argument, and ask every question." Some lawyers exaggerate this professional zeal. I prepared for a car accident trial once with the help of a newbie lawyer (yes, Harold again) who took that "ask every question" part rather seriously. In preparing the client, he asked him, "And sir, what was your licence plate number?"

I interrupted, asking him why he thought this question was relevant. He looked at me incredulously and said, "Ho ho, it demonstrates to the jury the client's credibility."

Actually, we managed to settle the case. I always wondered whether we could have fared better at trial. Maybe a jury would have concluded, "The plaintiff remembered his plate number. He's certainly credible. Let's add a couple of zeroes."

Maybe another reason for lawyers seemingly complicating matters is fear of malpractice, even in non-litigation situations. One colleague, Marvin, once represented a client who was purchasing a cottage in a very rural Northern Ontario area. The boondocks on steroids. The wilderness-loving client was gung-ho to obtain this lakefront property.

Unfortunately for the client the complication here was Marvin's thoroughness. His title search disclosed that the property was subject to a right of way registered in 1894 in favour of something like the no-longer-in-existence-for-over-a-century Great Canadian Northern Railway. The property had been transferred numerous times since then no problem, except for Marvin. He spent a fair bit of time ardently presenting his concerns to the client.

Reluctantly she backed out of the deal. No doubt she took Marvin's concerns seriously as presumably she did not want to be enjoying a suntan session when suddenly she hears a loud train whistle. She gets approached by a train engineer in striped overalls who says, "Ahem Madam, we're coming through. Please move that hammock."

After the client related this story, I chatted with Marvin, suggesting he may have been overdoing due diligence. His insightful response was reminiscent of the fine Charles Dickens language of *Oliver Twist*'s Mr. Bumble, who said, "The law is an ass." Actually, Marvin was saying, "Just being cautious. If anything happens, she will come after my ass, not yours." I suppose he was right there.

Lawyers also use confusing and excessive terms including but not limited to "hereinafters," "whereases," and of course, "including but not limited tos." It's all too much, *pater noster*.

But in my experience, lawyers often have difficulties properly estimating the time required to conduct a matter. I don't know what happened in the Lord Bacon case. Likely, from my experience, the trial coordinator probably reached out to the two lawyers for a reasonable time estimate.

Trial Coordinator: "Counsel, how long do you expect this matter to take?"

Plaintiff's Lawyer: "I'd say we should be done in a day. Easy."

Defendant's Lawyer: "The facts are not even in dispute. We should be over by the morning recess. I'll be short."

Plaintiff's Lawyer: "I agree with my learned friend. I'll be even shorter."

Perhaps many lawyers are imperfect time managers, but we can also cast blame on some judges. I knew a stern judge once who could not hear a matter without interrupting it with wiseacre quotes. On a guilty plea, after hearing the prosecutor's colourful summary of the offence, he would rattle off some Shakespeare, like Macbeth's "Double, double toil and trouble, fire burn and cauldron bubble." It did not lengthen the proceedings much; however, it did make some other lawyers in the courtroom rethink their intentions and ask for an adjournment. Depending on the judge's quote, to adjourn the case would, in Dickens's words, have been "a far, far better thing …"

Some judges cause delays in the system or even damage by, for want of another term, being nitpicking sticklers with the law. Actually, there is not want of another term. There is a term; they're being anal.

They can get carried away with unwarranted and unexplained jargon or rulings. I once witnessed a judge who seemed distracted a bit (this was not that same Shakespeare-quoting judge) erroneously give a man ninety days in jail despite the Crown Attorney (prosecutor) agreeing with defence counsel to a fine. The Crown immediately rose to make further submissions to honour the deal, pleading for a fine, but the judge smugly said, "I see. However, I cannot change my ruling. I'm *functus officio*."

Both lawyers, trying to regain their composure, made brief comments to the judge to reconsider his decision. As well, the man's wife jumped up and pleaded that her husband was the breadwinner of the family of five children. The scene reminded me of *Les Misérables*, where Jean Valjean gets whacked for about twenty years consequent to stealing a loaf of bread.

The gentleman's lawyer, who almost had cardiac arrest, tried explaining to his shocked client that *functus officio* was a nice Latin phrase, meaning the judge's mandate is over and he cannot reconsider, though he probably could have but thought he couldn't. The lawyer's subsequent translation for the wife of the phrase did not console her much. I for one did not expect her to say, "Of course, now I get it. *Functus officio*, that's the law. Oh well."

I doubt this incident, witnessed by a courtroom full of people, elevated respect for the law. To the judge, functus did trumpus justice. Nobody ever said access to justice was perfect. Not Lord Bacon. And certainly not Mr. Bumble.

CHAPTER FIVE

Fear of Lawyers:
You're a Lawyer. Lawyers Scare Me

"First let's kill all the lawyers."
~ William Shakespeare

Indeed, lawyers aren't perfect. We know what the public's general sentiments are about the profession. Actually, Shakespeare per se was not suggesting we kill all the lawyers. This quote is from the bard's play *Henry VI*, uttered by a villain Dick the Butcher who was provoking an insurrection and who wanted to do away with lawyers as being the instruments of justice—they would stand in his way. Shakespeare actually saw them as the frontline defenders of democracy. Fast forwarding to the present, you might call lawyers democracy's first responders. (Now you guys can leisurely write those LSATs.)

However, although we may not be threatened or damned, I would say the public is actually afraid of lawyers. Is this a good thing? It is if it keeps some people honest. Or as my daughter Natalie would say, "Nice!"

And what is there to be afraid of? How does this fear originate? Most of us have little or no contact with lawyers during our childhood. It's not like the experience most of us go through as kids, going to the doctor at a young age and getting poked by a long needle. I have yet to hear of a fifth grader booking an appointment with a lawyer so he can get his Will done in order to prevent his siblings and parents fighting over his baseball card collection in case something happens to him.

My first communication with a lawyer was as a teenager in Montreal after visiting a dentist. No, it was not a case of malpractice. He fixed a filling and sent us a bill for $25.00. My father, a humble tailor who earned not much more than that per week, thought the bill was outrageous. We sent the dentist a cheque for $12.50. My dad reasoned going 50-50 was fair.

This seemingly equitable offering did not sit well with the good dentist. He telephoned us and spoke to my father. A heated conversation ensued. I don't recall it all but I do remember my dad telling the dentist to wait a minute while he lit up a cigarette. After this necessary interlude, he told the dentist he would not rip him off like this were he to alter his pants.

We thought we were done.

However, shortly thereafter we received a letter from a Jacobsen, Samuels and Lafleur (or something law firm looking like that) saying Dr. Silverman retained them to recover a debt of $12.50. In addition, they claimed $15.00 for the cost of the letter.

Uncertain what all this meant, we took it to our rabbi who explained to us that this was a "lawyer's letter." He said they are demanding a total of $27.50 and if we don't pay it they may take us to court.

My father was not shaken or alarmed. He lit up his cigarette and said to the rabbi that if he ends up in court, he would tell the judge he was a World War 2 veteran and a good Canadian citizen and that $12.50 was more than fair to fix one small tooth. It sounded like a good legal argument to me. My dad obviously had a natural sense of the concept of *quantum meruit*.

My father was a fair man. He also offered the rabbi a cigarette.

After further discussion with the rabbi about the potential hazards of litigation, my dad reluctantly agreed to offer the dentist $5.00 additional. We had the rabbi relay the offer and fortunately it was actually accepted. In retrospect I wondered why they settled for $5.00 out of a $27.50 claim. Maybe they were spiritual, afraid of the ramifications of rattling the rabbi. Who knows?

My father was impressed by the lawyer's claiming $15.00 "just for writing a letter." He said he would have to take in a couple of pairs of trousers to earn that type of money. He added that he hoped the extra $5.00 would go to the lawyers, not the dentist. He also told me to consider becoming a lawyer, saying these guys can "squeeze you like a lemon." I took serious note of his wisdom. And here we are.

Actually, lawyers do generally get treated with deference. I found whenever I used to call a doctor's office on a case, dropping my professional standing often got me a quick response (as we well should).

True we usually get a voicemail message saying something like, "We're busy right now. If this is a medical emergency call 911. Otherwise please leave a message, you peasant." (OK, I exaggerate, but often judging by the gatekeeper's smug tone, you can readily infer that part about the peasant.)

However, the response is different when I leave a message saying something like "I am the lawyer for George Bentley, regarding the malpractice matter," I get a speedy return. Their voice message may as well say, "And if you're a lawyer calling, please press two. The doctor is in surgery. But then again, the patient won't mind; he's asleep anyway."

I actually had a treating specialist physician who said to me, "You're a lawyer. Lawyers scare me."

I thought he was joking. Then one day I sent him a letter on my office letterhead with some questions about the dubious treatment options he was suggesting for me. His reaction was to write to my family doctor who referred me to him, noting he could no longer keep me as a patient as he felt threatened. I have no clue why. I didn't even demand $15.00 for my letter.

I found at times of controversy it often does help to let people know you're a lawyer. Recently my good wife opened a can of sockeye salmon and noticed what looked like glass fragments. Fortunately, she did not ingest any. She sent an email to the company's customer service department and they replied that these glass-looking pieces were actually "struvites," namely transparent harmless chemical compounds common in canned fish. They thanked her for bringing this matter to their attention noting that customer feedback helps them serve the public better. They trusted she would continue to enjoy their salmon. They offered no compensation. This did not sit well with me.

Though retired from practice, I brushed off my armour. I sent the company an email saying that most people have never heard of struvites. The stuff looked like glass to us, and almost ingesting same is a good recipe for alarm and distress, anxiety, and mental shock. I added "I trust we need not escalate the matter." I signed it Marcel Strigberger, "barrister, solicitor and avocat."

Within a day or two I received a reply from the company's risk management office. They apologized for any inconvenience saying that though the struvites are safe to ingest, they were prepared to make amends by sending us a $100 voucher for Costco or Walmart along with a case of sockeye salmon. They also trusted we will continue to enjoy their salmon.

This was not good enough for me. I wanted more. I expected them to say something like, "We do not take product complaints seriously. We usually brush off all complainants. However, if we hear from a lawyer, that's different. We listen."

My good wife suggested we don't push it. We accepted their offer. But I know for sure the "barrister, solicitor, avocat" part propelled them into action.

Mark Twain said, "Always do the right thing. It will gratify some people and astonish the rest." Maybe this is why the public might be apprehensive about lawyers. Because in this imperfect world, we aim to let right prevail. It may rub some people the wrong way. Who knows? It did Dick the Butcher.

Meanwhile I am pleased to say we are indeed enjoying those complimentary cans of sockeye salmon.

CHAPTER SIX

Why Did the Lawyer Cross the Road? Are Lawyers Sometimes Chicken?

"Things done well and with a care are exempt of fear."
~ William Shakespeare

It's obvious Shakespeare never practised law. As lawyers, our work can get stressful, gripping us with fear. This must be a relevant issue as my Thesaurus notes at least three synonyms for fear beginning just with the letter "A" alone, namely "anxious," "alarmed," and "aghast."

Can an exploration of fear help us in our practices? Napoleon in describing military genius said something like, "The true genius is the one who can do the average thing when those around him grow hysterical with emotion and fright."

And isn't a litigation a type of warfare? Lawyers are the soldiers. And here in Canadian courts we even wear uniforms, donning black robes and white tabs. In England the barristers also in addition sport those wigs. I can see how this bellicose attire can frighten the enemy even more.

We often hear the comment, "A trial is not a tea party." Then again, some trials might indeed remind us of a tea party, namely *Alice in Wonderland*'s Mad Hatter's tea party.

I was in criminal court once waiting to be called when the case before mine involved some firearms offence. As the accused was testifying, the judge, having a reputation for being bizarre, took hold of the pistol in question and started playing with it, seemingly oblivious to the testimony. Defence counsel said to the judge, "Your Honour, I am not sure you are catching all of the evidence."

The judge became livid and adjourned the case, telling the lawyer he is considering charging him with contempt. His Honour reminded me not only of the Mad Hatter but also of the Queen of Hearts, who goes around shouting, "Off with their heads." The madness of some judges can certainly generate fear in the lawyers. I'm sure that poor lawyer felt aghast.

We have other sources of fear. One is missing limitations, or procedural deadlines. A common one here is the two years one has to issue a claim post-accident. Some lawyers still miss limitation dates. Or they almost miss them but raise their blood pressure catching it at the last minute, as follows: Toronto's time zone is Eastern Standard time. However, the Western Ontario city of Kenora is in the Central Time Zone. A lawyer from Kenora once spoke at a seminar here in Toronto, noting he sometimes gets frantic calls late in the afternoon from EST lawyers who realize their claims are in their eleventh hour. They provide basic details of their case and the Kenora lawyer has that extra hour to get the claim done and issued at his local courthouse. Phew!

I actually took his business card only to keep it pinned on the cork board in my office where I collected funny cartoons. It often served to remind me not to leave important matters to the last minute. I actually scribbled on it an image of a character with halo and wings. It added to the chuckles the cartoons gave me to ease any tensions whenever I needed a humour fix.

Which gets us to clients. Can they strike fear in the lawyer? Actually, they can be a bigger source of fear than mad judges, procedural hurdles, or even nasty lawyer opponents. I'll have more to say about clients soon, including the good, the bad, and the impossible.

I would often worry they would blow the case. For example, in preparing for a personal-injury examination for discovery, we would instruct the client to be conservative when asked how severe the symptoms were on a scale of one to ten. At the office rehearsal, the client would say something like six to eight. Notwithstanding, at the examination, when asked, a number of clients would blurt out an ugly three-letter word, "Ten." Sometimes they would top this answer up when asked if they ever felt better since the accident, replying emphatically, "Never."

Given that fees on these files were on a contingency percentage basis, I would feel as though I was personally writing out a cheque to the insurance company.

Are there ways of dealing with these fears? Some literature suggests the anxiety is often caused by catastrophizing a situation. If the event makes you feel as though your case is sinking like the Titanic, just say to yourself something like, "Worst case scenario, it's only money." Does that help? It might to a certain extent but I'm not so sure how well that works when it's your own money. My mood would start going south when once again I would see myself writing out that cheque to that insurance company.

Then there are the classical bromides of solace. Words such as "Everything happens for a reason" sounds OK until you ask, "Why is it happening to me? Give me a good reason." A good break in the form of a brisk walk can be helpful to break the fear pattern. I would often saunter out for a half hour or so after lunch, at times walking through a nearby old cemetery. Aside from the exercise, I found it a relaxing switch to go from reading nasty threatening emails to eyeballing some tombstone inscriptions. When reading something like "Arthur Appleby, born March 20, 1911, died October 13, 2002," I found it cleared the head a bit. I realized that unlike the occupants of this venue, I still had choices. This is important as with a clear head you can perhaps do the average thing like Napoleon said. If in a pickle, you might just think about calling that lawyer in Kenora.

As lawyers we are engaged in battle with a colleague who also thinks he or she is right. Can we banish fear? And need we banish it totally? Perhaps we can take some comfort in the wise words of Mark Twain, who said, "Courage is resistance to fear, mastery of fear—not absence of fear. It's OK to sometimes feel chicken.

And now, as promised, let me say something about the clients.

CHAPTER SEVEN: PART 1

Send In the Clients—Yeah

"A kiss is just a kiss, a sigh is just a sigh. The fundamental things apply."
~ Sam in the movie *Casablanca*

For lawyers in practice, the fundamental thing is the client. The law is just the law but the practice thereof is still a business. As such, if you have a practice, having clients is helpful. However, how does one land them? They certainly don't teach you in law school how to attract clients. But let me share some thoughts from my journey, or rather, as Homer might say, my odyssey (not Homer Simpson).

After law school I presumed my legal career was set to fly as I scored A's in contacts, torts, and evidence. Okay, I barely scraped through international law. Nobody is perfect. But then again, I never cared much about representing some country like Denmark in a possible international dispute with Japan over fishing rights.

Initially, I worked briefly at a big law firm that boasted blue-chip clients, including one of Canada's major banks that had been around since before Confederation when Canada became a dominion in 1867.

Interestingly, they made me sign a non-competition agreement not to poach their clients in the event that I left. Supposedly they feared that I might one day open my own practice in some storefront and invite the world-class bank's CEO for coffee and entice him to move its business to me. A tempting thought. These big law firms think of everything. However, I probably would have to be careful not to let on that my knowledge of the law was a bit below perfection as I almost flunked international law.

I soon opened my solo practice, with trepidation. My first big break came early on right after my number-one son, Daniel, was born. I went to a local drug store to buy some Pampers and I struck up a conversation with Harry, the pharmacist. He told me he was not happy with his lawyer, noting the guy usually delayed returning his messages. He was now looking for a new lawyer who "will give me five-star service."

Given that I had some available down time then, I assured him my specialty was promptly returning calls. I had no doubt I could deliver on this assurance. Harry did not ask nor did I tell him about my skimpy knowledge of international law. He soon sent me some decent business. I can't talk numbers, but I did say to myself, I no longer have to consider going after that bank CEO. That road not taken. Alas!

I did however have to butter Harry somewhat by continuing to buy all those Pampers from him even though they were overpriced there. I guess circumstances drive our marketing methods. Some lawyers take their target clients golfing, others send them NHL hockey tickets, and still others buy their Pampers.

As a sole practitioner managing a fledgling practice, I generally had to take on most of whatever work came along, and some of it was spooky scary. I recall a collection case where my client retained me to recover a sizable debt from a shady grocer, Jocko, in a seedy area of town. I sent a demand letter to the grocer. Jocko soon telephoned me and invited me to come over to his store where he said he would personally give me the cash. This invite sounded suspicious to me. Why did he want to meet me personally and in his lair? I would have been content for him to simply tell me he is mailing me a cheque. With hesitation I mustered up some courage and accepted his invitation. Given the questionable area of town, I decided to take the bus to the store. I heard there had been a rash of car thefts in the area and I did not want to risk anything happening to my Toyota Corolla.

As I entered the store, I felt like one half of the Hansel and Gretel team. I asked myself whether this "gingerbread house" was worth the risk. Jocko greeted me with a smile and a handshake. I thought to myself, "a sheep in wolf's clothing." The gentleman then asked that I accompany him to the basement. Uh oh! I hesitantly did so without knowing what might be waiting for me. I was glad this was not Valentine's Day. And unlike that warehouse in Chicago, the police would never find me here.

The basement was dimly lit and musty. The place resembled my vision of the Bastille—before it was stormed in 1789. I almost expected to hear the anguished cry of prisoners screaming, "Hey, we're here. Help. Grab that torch." I noticed what looked like an arch-shaped tunnel entrance. I wondered whether it led to the local sewer system. I thought to myself that if in the pinch and I have to bolt, I could venture through it. Victor Hugo's *Les Misérables* came to mind. I started to commiserate with Jean Valjean. Here I am representing a client and wading through the sewer system of Toronto. And there behind me in hot pursuit is Jocko shouting, "J'accuse."

As my life to date flashed through my mind, I wondered whether it was a mistake to have left Big Law. Certainly, that bank would never have sent me on this type of mission. My adrenalin was rushing like Old Faithful. Jocko opened a drawer to an old desk and reached in. I said to myself, "here it comes." To my great relief he delivered the cash. And to boot he even offered me a Pepsi. I took it.

I reported this service to my client. He was very pleased and promised to send me more collection cases. I almost viewed this promise as a threat.

And so, what did I generally do to generate business? One popular advertisement resource was a bus-stop bench ad. Not cheap. I sprung for one bench near a hospital hoping to attract personal injury cases. The problem was that waiting passengers would sit on the bench, thereby blocking the message. I would pass by and was aghast that these people were so inconsiderate. I felt like shouting, "Hey, get your ass off my bench."

I think about it all now and am grateful that I had a comfortable practice. But what qualities, tricks, or traits helped? You may be surprised. A client once told me what he admired about me the most was that I was humble. I was certainly surprised. Who knows? Then again, if I admit I'm humble am I proving him wrong? Is this admission a sign of conceit? Other clients would say they were most impressed with my promptly returning their messages. I guess this habit I acquired out of involuntary circumstances stuck after leaving Big Law.

What else worked for me? Deploying your God-given sense of humour always helps. You need not tell jokes. I simply had a humour board on my wall with cute notes such as *Far Side* cartoons; bizarre news clippings; and quotes from Einstein, Churchill, and Mark Twain. Clients usually found looking at it pleasantly distracting. And it did help melt away the image of stiffness many people have about lawyers. At worst, humour will help manage your blood pressure. And maybe your adrenalin. You never know when you might have to spend some spooky moments somewhere subterranean.

Also, as I speak French, I attracted a fair number of Francophones. Actually, one client who had a claim against a large fast-food outfit after finding a bug in his pizza, retained me as he just liked the name Marcel. I mention this as some colleagues might perhaps consider a name change to Marcel. You never know whether this move might land you that next client who ingests a bug lodged in their pizza. There might just be a pattern here.

And speaking of languages, Toronto, where I practised, is one of the world's most multicultural cities. A veritable United Nations of people. As a result, my clients were very eclectic, originating from all six continents. I say six as I never had a client who came from Antarctica. My loss no doubt.

As a result of having this mix of clients, I often picked up on their languages and I'm sure they generally appreciated my efforts to understand their native tongues. One of my greater joys while in my litigation practice was representing these colourful clients. The beauty of this was that I have learned many words from diverse languages. I concluded that there really is not that much difference in the languages. After all, English does stem from a number of languages, some ancient. For example, I once interviewed a Greek lady who slipped and fell on ice. Her English was poor and her son George accompanying her was translating. Naturally, it was all Greek to me but soon I started picking up words and phrases. At one point I asked the mother how she slipped. She went on at length in Greek, waving one hand up and around and ending with the words, "Just like that." I asked her son to translate and he related the graphic details of the event concluding that down she went, "just like that."

Somehow, I was able to figure this last phrase out. I was proud of myself. I asked the lady about the injury and she pointed to her head speaking a number of seemingly unintelligible Greek words. With diligent listening, however, I was able to understand one phrase she uttered: "A big backache, that's it." I looked at George and he translated that she fell backwards and that she was suffering from a big backache. I told him proudly that I thought that I had picked up on that phrase as it sounded amazingly similar to English. George advised that much of the English language originates from Greek. We both agreed that indeed with a bit of desire and effort anybody speaking English could pick up Greek in no time. To ensure that I would actually learn as much Greek as I could, I decided to write all these newly learned words and phrases into a journal. I noted, "Just like that," and "a big backache, that's it" into my journal.

A while later I settled a motor-vehicle claim for an elderly Punjabi gentleman. He did not speak one word of English and he was accompanied by his grandson/translator, Jagdeep. I told Jagdeep I would be in touch when funds arrive. Unfortunately, delivery of funds was delayed and two weeks later I received a phone call from my client himself. He uttered his name and in Punjabi he said the word, "Cheque?" I did not know what to do as my knowledge of Punjabi failed me. Actually, I do not speak a word of Punjabi. But where there is a will there is a way. I listened carefully as he repeated the word supplemented by a further couple of Punjabi words: "Cheque come yet?" I said to him, "Jagdeep home?" My diligent attempt at Punjabi worked. A minute later Jagdeep took the line. I told him about my comprehension predicament and he conferred with my client and translated, "Is the cheque here yet?"

Uh huh! That's exactly what I suspected he was saying. I told Jagdeep that there was definitely some similarity between English and Punjabi. He agreed that perhaps the lengthy British presence in India may have forged this similarity. Who knows?

I took out my journal and penned in the words, "In Punjabi, 'cheque come yet' means, 'Is the cheque here yet?'" I was elated. I felt I could soon switch careers and get a job with Duolingo.

Pretty soon I found no language whatsoever a barrier to my communicating with clients. I had a Mandarin-speaking client who was not too successful in a real estate litigation case and not too happy with my account. A cousin acted as translator. When I suggested to them what I thought was a reasonable compromise for my bill, the two of them conferred and the client rattled off his response in Mandarin, ending with the words, "No way."

I sensed I was on to something. Maybe I picked up on the intonation. I looked at the interpreter and asked for a translation. He told me my offer was not acceptable. Bingo! I had now learned a phrase in Mandarin as well. I opened my journal and jotted down my newly learned phrase in Mandarin. "No way" means "not acceptable." Actually, the cousin added of his own accord the words "Full Stop." I did not enter this phrase in my journal as that of course isn't Mandarin. The good thing is we did amicably resolve my account and the client agreed to send me more money the next week.

During the course of this relationship, I learned yet another Mandarin phrase. After four weeks had rolled by without seeing his payment, I called the client. The gentleman uttered a few words in Mandarin ending with the words, "Cheque in mail, goodbye."

Unfortunately, there was nobody around to translate that one for me. I bit my pencil as I was about to make a journal entry. Could it mean what I thought it meant? As another two weeks rolled by uneventfully, I could only presume that indeed he was telling me that the cheque was in the mail. This presumption was bolstered by the fact that I noticed a bit of a similarity between this comment and that of the Punjabi gentleman. The word "cheque" has similar connotations in both Mandarin and Punjabi. And it was best characterized as an item the delivery of which is often delayed. I spoke to that Mandarin interpreter who confirmed that very translation.

Isn't it amazing that there are even some common links between words in Mandarin and Punjabi? To think it all started with the Tower of Babel. As the scripture reads in Genesis, Chapter 1, Verse 9, "That is why it was called Babel, because there the Lord confused the language of the world. From there the Lord scattered them over the face of the whole earth."

Incredible! Aren't we all from a common origin? And with a bit of effort, we can readily understand and get along with one another. It's a small world after all. And it's also good for business. As I said initially, they don't teach you in law school how to attract clients. I will say we will all travel our own individual journey, or perhaps odyssey. Bon voyage.

But as much as we need clients, can they sometimes be a problem?

CHAPTER SEVEN: PART 2

Send the Client Packing—Uggh!

"It seems, after all that there are no nonpeculiar people."
~ Saul Bellow

Clients: yeah or uggh? My learned mentor, Hank, used to say, "The biggest problem in practice is getting clients. The second biggest is dealing with them." How true. After forty-plus years in the trenches, I'll continue to say emphatically that clients can generate more aggravations than tough opposing counsel, difficult judges, or even technology, the latter which in my practice was generally frightening and confrontational. But that is a story for another chapter. You can laugh at me more in Chapter Twenty-Five. One problem at a time.

What is a client? The word "client" probably comes from some Latin word, *cliens*, which likely means, "OK lawyer. You're mine."

Unlike other relationships, a lawyer-client obligation can spawn without the lawyer even consenting to it. We are warned to beware of the "phantom client." The Ontario Rules of Professional Conduct say in short that X is your client if he has consulted you and either retained you or has "a reasonable expectation that he retained you." Thus, dropping some legal gems at a party about how you would fix the clock of that nasty insurance company, denying the listener's claim can potentially expose the lawyer to liability.

He or she may call one day to chat further, and then you discover the limitation or deadline date to act on the matter is past due. The "client" asks why the lawyer did not tell him about the deadline that evening at Marge and Albert's wedding. "Hey lawyer, after that chat while we were munching on sushi, I had a reasonable expectation that I had retained you."

The only broken clock the lawyer may have to fix now is his own.

This phantom client is a lawyer's albatross. You don't see it with other professions or callings. I can't imagine some guy sitting at the opera and suddenly his tooth pops out. He calls the dentist saying, "Remember when we stood in line at McDonalds, we struck up a conversation and I mentioned my tooth felt funny, well, you never told me this could happen." The dentist can easily brush the guy off. He has no McProblem.

The lawyer on the other hand may have to report this potential malpractice claim by the phantom client to his or her Errors and Omissions (E & O) insurer.

Then we have the lawyer's obligation to avoid a conflict of interest. I knew a rogue husband who was a physician who knew the rules, and in order to limit his wife's choice of top-gun family lawyers, hastily called several of them to chat for a few minutes. When the wife eventually approached these lawyers, her call rang a bell, and predictably they all responded with something like, "Oh, you're the wife of that dermatologist who called us claiming you moonlight as a dominatrix. Sorry."

Any hint of a conflict of interest and the lawyer has to back off. This does not make sense to me at all. I think it would be much more economical if we could indeed represent both sides to a dispute. Wouldn't this result in a quicker and cheaper resolution?

Or how about one individual representing four sides of a dispute? I have added a fantasy tale at the end of this chapter about one person being both plaintiff and defendant and the lawyer for each. The story is entitled "Me, and Me and My RRSP." Nothing like a four-ring circus.

And speaking of pain, once you do get properly retained, you really have to watch your back. And I am not talking about that dominatrix.

The Difficult Client

Our E & O insurer warns us of "the difficult client." There are a number of tell-tale signals of the difficult client.

1. The lawyer switcher

You are potential lawyer number four. The client will point out the faults of lawyers one, two, and three, but you have to question if indeed all the other lawyers delayed handling his case as they were all out constantly playing golf. You have to be even more careful if the client tells you he likes you; you're different. Red flag!

2. The excessively demanding client

This client assumes that your case portfolio consists of one file: his. He'll call frequently, commenting, "When's the trial? It's been a week already since you took on the case." The best you can say to them is that this isn't a television show. These cases take more than an hour to conclude. Or the client will say, "My neighbour's niece got three million dollars with her lawyer for her injury. And she only hurt her thumb. That's not as serious as a pinky."

You get the picture. The good thing in dealing with these clients is that you can tell them to retain their neighbour's lawyer. Even help them find just the right lawyer by Googling with them something like, "injuries … million dollars settlement … specialist pinky lawyer."

3. The client who gives you money problems

To some clients, what does paying your lawyer have to do with the price of a cappuccino at Starbucks? I would beware of clients who give you some of the following responses when you ask for funding.

- Don't worry about the money.
- This case is not about dollars; it's about principles.
- I always pay my bills. Just ask my cousin Iggy.

In rating the relevance of paying their lawyer, they generally subscribe to the Latin maxim of *de minimis*. This means too trivial to merit consideration. If you overlook this, you may be subscribing to the Latin maxim of *pro bono*. Experience taught me to enter both these phrases in that language journal. (OK, more Latin but at least I'm translating it.)

4. *The Uncooperative client*

Do they exist? Grrr. I am talking about the clients who are generally unreachable. They'll vanish without notifying their lawyer. I actually experienced these too often, and in the midst of cases where I was heavily invested in disbursements. I had already paid out thousands for experts' reports. The clients just evaporated. My letters were returned. One client had an email address but my emails to him may as well have bounced back reading: "I'll respond soon. I'm out sailing my boat near the Bermuda Triangle." My efforts to track him down were futile. I even couldn't get any help from his cousin Iggy.

Then there are the clients who simply do not provide you with the documents you need. They'll say something like, "You'll have it all on Tuesday." I'm not sure how to say that in Latin but the general translation is, "If you believe that then you'll also believe this year the Toronto Maple Leafs will win the Stanley Cup."

Dumping the Client

There comes a time when you have to terminate the relationship. Like the Von Trapps merrily sang in the movie, "So long, farewell, auf Wiedersehen, goodnight." Unfortunately, the solution is not that simple. It would be great if lawyers could just sever the lawyer-client relationship via email.

But unfortunately, we need a court order to break the shackles. And to succeed you must swear an affidavit showing justifiable cause. However, you need to maintain lawyer-client confidentiality lest an opposing lawyer finds out about your tribulations.

The phrase of choice is, "I respectfully ask this honourable court to remove me as lawyer of record as I have not been able to get proper instructions from my client." And so, if when you ask for some money and the client emails you an emoji of a wide grin smiley, or the client asks you whether it was obvious to you that he faked his injuries, or if he attends at your office unexpectedly, wearing a costume of the Grim Reaper and terrifies your staff, your affidavit will have to be modified a bit, to read, "I respectfully ask this honourable court to remove me as lawyer of record as I have not been able to get proper instructions from my client."

Most judges will pick up from the desperation in your voice and know what you mean and not press you for details. Some will no doubt probably say, "Certainly counsel, I get it; Grim Reaper."

Occasionally the lawyer lucks out and the difficult client bolts, saving the lawyer the need to get that court order removing him from the record. Are the lawyer's tribulations over? Glad you asked. Of course not. There is also a rule on getting unretained. Even if the client dismisses you, you still have to write to the client to confirm you are no longer acting. So, if a client says to you, "You are an incompetent cretin of a scumbag shyster; you're fired," you have to respond in writing: "Dear Sir, This will confirm your instructions that I no longer represent you." Otherwise, you might still be this fan's lawyer. Oh yes, and getting back to the lawyer's strict duty of confidentiality, we are to maintain confidentiality even if someone threatens to put bamboo strips up our fingernails. This duty extends even to that guy we just met at Marge and Albert's wedding.

I think we would all like to see an end to this senseless onus. I say, for example, if a client does not pay our fees in a timely manner, we should be free to tell the world. We should be allowed to post it on Facebook. Isn't that more equitable than having to get off the record and then have to chase the bum through a legal action, thereby taking up our court's precious resources?

We can just post online, "My client, Gordon William McKnish, residing in Richmond Hill, owes me $4,000 for all the hard work I did for him and he is stiffing me." Actually, McKnish is not a real client. I say that in the event that there is actually a Gordon William McKnish in Richmond Hill, that he realizes that I selected that name totally randomly. So, to you William Gordon McKnish of Richmond Hill, if you exist, you are not my client and you do not owe me a penny. If, however, you want to give me $4,000, I'll take it.

But until some of these rules change, the lawyer's recourse to getting paid is to either sue the client or apply to the court to have the bill assessed by an assessment officer. The latter process is a quicker more summary way of getting it done, but it is fraught with greater risk for the lawyer. This should be obvious as an "assessment of costs," as it is called, is a procedure most often launched by the client who does not like the bill.

It is like a trial before an assessment officer, not a judge, who listens with red pen in hand to the lawyer describe in detail all the services rendered to the client while said client sits in the courtroom appearing to be overwhelmed, having a baffled look on his face, which reads, "I didn't know lawyers actually charge for their services."

The assessment officer considers a number of key factors in the case, including the lawyer's expertise, time spent and complexities encountered, and results achieved. And then he ignores them all. Well, not really. It often just feels this way. The officer will generally praise the lawyer's work, but at the end of the day chop away at the figures. And on a bad day the officer can even make the lawyer pay some of the client's legal fees if applicable.

Again, I know of no other calling where such a scrutinizing resource for reviewing a bill is available to the client or customer. A plumber recently came to my house to unclog a sink. His bill was $264 being $99 for showing up and $165 for the fifteen minutes needed to do the unclogging by running a device called a snake down the drain. That works out to $1,056 per hour. And he did not even fully clean up the mess.

And what was my recourse to his hefty bill? Zero, nada, or as they say in Greek, "Bapkis." (That looks and sounds like an ancient Greek word. Maybe Aristotle used to munch on some at high tea.)

If there were a procedure in the plumbing trade similar to the bill assessment drill where clients can apply to get their lawyer's account reviewed and challenged, my case might unfold like this:

Assessment Officer:

I have listened to the evidence of both the plumber Joe of Joe's Plumbing, and the customer who claims the plumber's bill is outrageous. In reviewing the bill, I note that plumber Joe charged $99 for showing up, or as the customer claims, "just showing up." This effort by Joe should not be underestimated. In addition to enduring the risks of driving, the plumber had to park his van in the customer's driveway. He then had to undo his seatbelt. Then he had to exit the vehicle and remove his tools. There's more. The plumber noted he had to ring the customer's doorbell. Of course. I find that $99 is reasonable for the attendance. Check. Let me now consider the principles of assessing the plumber's bill.

1. *Plumber's expertise*

Joe has been doing plumbing for seven years following his graduation from the Eastern Seminary of Plumbing (ESOP), where he majored in faucets. He does general residential plumbing, though he says his preferred area of practice is drains. I find that this makes him a drain expert.

2. *Time spent*

Joe spent .25 hours unclogging the drain, and the Code of Tariff Charges (COTCH) allows a fee rate of $660 per hour for services rendered by a plumber at Joe's level of expertise. He asserts that it was a tough drain to unclog as it had clogged stuff down there. I agree.

3. *Complexities of the case*

Joe notes that he actually spent about .15 hours doing the unclogging but it took him one hour to struggle to remove that snake. He added that snakes can be unpredictable and as such they must be handled with extreme caution. I agree.

4. *Result achieved*

The customer conceded that at the end of the day the pesky drain was unclogged. He did complain that the plumber left a bit of a mess as some debris splashed onto the kitchen window. Joe reiterates that this was caused by that pesky snake. And in any event the mess was something that could readily be cleaned up with some Windex.

5. *Conclusion*

Taking all the requisite assessment factors into account, I find that Joe's account of $264 for plumbing services rendered in this very interesting case reasonable. Joe is now asking for an additional $200 for his time spent on this assessment, claiming the customer's move to assess were "egregious, frivolous, and vexatious." I think the plumber is overreaching somewhat. What's fair is fair. I will not allow any additional fees to Joe. After all, what does he want now, the kitchen sink?"

And so, was Hank correct in his assessment of the client? As they say in that noble dead language, "caveat lawyer." What say you?

As promised here at the end of this chapter is "Me, and Me, and My RRSP." CAVEAT: Don't try this at home.

Me, and Me, and My RRSP

For years now I have been kicking in thousands of dollars a year into a self-directed Registered Retirement Savings Plan (RRSP). And for years now (the same number actually), I have been trying to think of ingenious ways of getting the money back out without promptly paying tax.

A while back I bought a house and my accountant suggested that I could finally hit the fund, using the same to finance the purchase. The

catch, however, was that I would have to replenish the kitty with a mortgage and pay back the money monthly.

"Do you mean I would be both the mortgagor and mortgagee?" I
asked my accountant.

"Exactly. You pay the money to yourself. But it's an arm's length
mortgage. You must pay it monthly, come hell or high water—or my bill."

This sounded like a win-win situation. I busted my RRSP and placed
the mortgage on the house. I made the first couple of mortgage payments
no problem.

Unfortunately, the conflict of wearing two hats soon started heating
up. I received a whopping realty tax bill from the municipality. It was so
high that the amount apportioned to school taxes alone could have bought
all of Oxford University.

"There's no way I'm paying this," I said to myself. I missed the due
date and I felt good. It then hit me that the mortgage had a provision in it
that if the mortgagor fails to make a tax payment, he is in default and the
mortgagee can pay it and add the tab to the mortgage debt. That didn't
worry me.

As mortgagee, however, there was no way I was going to permit any
compromise to my retirement nest egg and I promptly made the payment.
I then sent the mortgagor a letter as follows:

Dear Mortgagor:
We have just paid the outstanding realty taxes that ought to have been
paid by you. We trust that this was just an oversight. Please don't let it
happen again or action will be taken against you.
Yours very truly,
The Mortgagee

When I received the letter, I was furious. "Stuff it!" I exclaimed, tear-
ing it to confetti. A few weeks later there was a leak in my basement. It was

apparent that major work was necessary. But funds were a bit tight and I had other matters to worry about than a dumb leaky basement.

As mortgagee, I just happened to peruse the mortgage and I noticed the provision whereby the mortgagee has a right to inspect the premises to make sure his investment is sound, and if the place needs repairs he can compel the mortgagor to fix it up.

Quite by chance I decided to go down to the basement to check on my security, and lo and behold—a flood. "How did that irresponsible duffer allow it to go this far?" I bellowed. I didn't even bother writing. I called in a contractor immediately and tacked the bill onto the mortgage debt. "I'm going to have to inspect this place more often in view of the slob living here," I told my wife.

For the next few months, the debtor and creditor lived in harmony, until one day I bought a new car and I wanted to defer my mortgage payments for a couple of months.

"The hell with that mortgagee," I said to myself. "What will he do if I don't pay? Take a pound of flesh?"

It was mid-month and as I was sitting at my office desk contemplating my fortune, I realized that I had not yet received my mortgage payment. I decided to call the mortgagor at home, and guess what, there was no answer. I was convinced I was dealing with a deadbeat and enough was enough. I decided to see a lawyer.

It occurred to me however that since I was a lawyer myself perhaps, under the circumstances, I could take a shortcut and handle the matter in-house. I might have a fool for a client, but who's going to tell? I fired off the following letter—by registered mail.

Dear Mr. Strigberger:
My client advises that once again you are in default. Monies now overdue must reach this office no later than 4 p.m. this Friday, failing which

foreclosure proceedings will be commenced against you without further notice. In addition, you must also include the sum of $100 for legal costs.

Yours truly,
Marcel Strigberger

I got home from a hard day at the office one day and what do I see in my mailbox? A notice indicating that there was a registered letter waiting for me at the post office. Now who would be sending me a registered letter I wondered?

I attended the postal clerk, who wanted to see some identification to make sure who I was. She then handed me the letter. She seemed puzzled as she put away my business card.

I noticed the envelope was from a law office. I opened it, read the letter, and hit the roof. "Foreclose me will he? I slaved for years to buy this house and to make a home for my wife and three lovely kiddies. Doesn't he care?"

The clerk asked me if there was a problem with the letter and after explaining it all to her, she went postal. She put on her hat and coat and ran out of the building.

I was livid. In view of my emotional state, I thought I had better see a lawyer. I then thought to myself, "what the heck." I made a call and the receptionist said that Mr. Strigberger could see me first thing tomorrow morning.

I got to the law office at 8:30 the next morning. Unfortunately, in my eagerness I had to wait a half hour as the office did not open until 9:00. At 9:01 I charged right past the receptionist into Strigberger's office and threw the letter on the desk. It was 9:02 when I was sitting behind my desk and noticed this very upset character barge into my office and throw a letter on my desk. I skimmed the letter and the urgency of the matter was apparent.

I told the client to relax and assured him that I would take the situation in hand. I firstly wanted to dispose of an important preliminary matter, and so I made a couple of comments. The client was not happy at all.

I came to the office for legal assistance and you won't believe this: Before taking on the case, Strigberger wanted a $1,000 retainer. He said something about it being novel. I stormed out of the office. "Let him foreclosure me all he wants," I said. I pondered the situation and realized that I would have the last laugh. I would rigorously defend any action brought, and come trial time I would pull the necessary strings to make sure the mortgagee and his lawyer would never show up in court.

CHAPTER EIGHT

Time: Yours, Mine, and Hours—
Billable of Course

"'The time has come,' the walrus said, 'to talk of many things: of
shoes and ships and ceiling wax ... and whether pigs have wings.'"
~ Lewis Carroll
Through the Looking Glass

This is also a good a time as any to discuss time. As we lawyers say,
"All we have to sell is our time." And I did say the practice of law is
a business?

I once had lunch with a colleague. I asked Leo to spend a few extra
minutes enjoying a second cup of tea. Leo, of my vintage, told me he bills
$350 per hour. He noted this second cup would take ten minutes to drink,
and ergo, it would cost him about sixty dollars.

Trying to mitigate the cost, I asked, "Leo, your partner gets
fifty percent?"

"Yeah, that's true," he agreed.

"So the tea will only run you $30," I reasoned.

He nodded his approval. I then added, "Of your income, you pay about fifty percent for taxes?" (This is Canada, not some relatively tax-free haven like the United States.)

"Uh hmm," he grunted.

"So it's really only costing you about $15 for that second cup?" (My Socratic reasoning was winning out, I felt.)

"But it would still cost me $1.50 for the tea."

I agreed. Added to the $15, this was a total of $16.50 for that second cup.

"And for me to earn $16.50 net after taxes, I've got to bill $33."

I couldn't have agreed more. We both noticed a student sitting nearby having a tea and presumably it was costing him only $1.50. (Oh, for those super student days!) Leo and I soon concurred that we would have to pay over twenty times this amount for that next cup of tea. We both envied that student.

I quickly took a sip of my first tea, and we both stormed out of the restaurant. As lawyers we have to be mindful of our time. And what is our routine unit of billing time? Point one of an hour; i.e., 1.

Is that metric? Not exactly as that works out to six minutes. Is it fair to the client? What if your phone conversation takes four minutes? You still bill for six? How would you like to go to an expensive chocolate store and the clerk puts a few premium truffles on the scale? They weigh 850 grams, but she charges you for 1,000 grams saying, "We sell these by the kilo. That's close enough." (I trust for anybody not familiar with metric, I need not convert these weights and measures into ounces. You get the picture). And unlike seeing the evidence on the scale, with a lawyer's bill the clients must rely on the honour system. This gets us back to having to trust your lawyer.

I knew a lawyer X who used to bill rather creatively. If he called someone and reached their voicemail, he would bill the client .1. If, say, the client returned his call and left him a voicemail, that was another .1.

Nothing was achieved for the client. That's like the chocolate store clerk saying, "Those truffles aren't available today. That will be $43 please."

I discovered X's billing practices during an account assessment I did for the client. (You all recall what that is.) The officer slashed X's bill big time, finding other irregular and unscrupulous time-padding, such as travel time to walk to the courthouse. I was so pleased with the assessment office's decision that I was tempted to get him a box of chocolate truffles. It probably would have been OK—and I would not have put it on my client's tab.

But we lawyers can also be bitten by our clients who don't value our time. A separated lady once pleaded to meet in the evening at her suburban house as she had two small children and it was hard for her to travel downtown to my office. I attended and spent two hours meeting her. Ultimately, she did not retain me. I sent her a bill, which she refused to pay, claiming "I thought this was just a 'getting to know you' meeting."

I thought this added a new dimension to lawyers' billable time. Does a house call and spending two hours giving the client legal advice have a value of zero? I certainly can't see this happening with other callings, like that plumber. Imagine some magnanimous plumber coming to your house and spending two hours installing a toilet.

Customer: "What do I owe you sir?"

Plumber: "No charge madam. This was just a getting-to-know-your-bathroom visit."

I could have pursued her further and assessed my account. I doubt that the assessment officer would have concluded, "I'm not allowing these two hours. Pure gouging. After all, what did the lawyer do for the client? This was just a getting-to-know-you meeting."

At this point, especially given that I am retired from practice, maybe I should mention Lady X's name. To hell with confidentiality. Bah! Her name: Lady X.

Lawyers' fees have come a long way. As I noted earlier, in ancient Rome legal fees were originally banned. In other words, lawyers earned about what I did with that aforementioned lady. Fortunately, Emperor Claudius lifted the ban. Hail Claudius! But caveat, lawyers' bills had that ceiling of ten thousand sesterces. But before you say wow, a Wikipedia entry reads, "This was not much money. It was a few pieces of silver," which likely could not get a hard-working and deserving lawyer two red seats in the Coliseum to watch a good gladiator match.

The Satires of Juvenal complained that there was no money in working as an advocate. That's exactly how I felt after that just-getting-to-know-you meeting. At least she had access to justice, albeit *pro bono*.

And unlike doctors, lawyers generally respect our clients' time, rarely keeping them waiting. Doctors on the other hand waste our time deliberately. I'm certain all first-year medical students take a mandatory course called "Waiting 101." It's probably in their oath. I Googled "Hippocrates patient's time relevant," and what came up was, "Hang on and take a seat. Read a magazine."

We also don't waste our time sleeping. A U.S. federal survey noted that lawyers sleep seven hours per night. Doctors sleep more than lawyers, logging seven hours and two minutes. I'd say the doctors just pretend to sleep this additional time to keep us waiting two extra minutes.

I am retired from practice now, and I certainly enjoy the luxury of that second leisurely cup of tea. I wish I had allowed myself that well-spent indulgence back then more often. I certainly wouldn't miss the $33 now.

CHAPTER NINE

Lawyers' Lairs: Does Size Matter? Big Law, Small Law, La La La

"If size mattered, the elephant would be king of the jungle."
~ Rickson Gracie, Brazilian mixed martial artist

Now that we have heard all kinds of comments about lawyers, the next question is, how do lawyers provide their services? Let me talk about the law firm. Does size matter? Let's start big.

BigLaw!
What is BigLaw? I consulted one of my most trusted word reference texts, the *Urban Dictionary*. This wise opus defines BigLaw as "a collection of huge law firms in major cities (particularly NYC) where thousands of Ivy Leaguers and honour students make six-figure salaries straight out of law school. They usually quit after a couple of years of virtual slavery, but if they stay in the game, they end up running the country."

I suppose my years of solo practice would fall short of BigLaw. Actually, after a few weeks in, I shed all aspirations of running the country.

Canada's loss. Incidentally, I Googled "SmallLaw" but all I saw was "Small Law." Alas, not helpful. Small was a lawyer's name. Stanley Small.

I started to think what it would have been like to work in a mega law-yer firm. A few subtle differences. Firstly, partnership? After my brief stint with BigLaw, I started my own practice and I climbed this ladder quickly. I did not have to work double shifts to become a partner. I did not have to wine and dine any potential clients. My boss elevated me to the rank of general "badda bing badda boom." Not bad for someone straight out of McGill Law School, non *magna cum laude* (and a lousy mark in interna-tional law).

And speaking of struggles, BigLaw associates often do work up to seventy to eighty hours/week, arriving at 7 a.m. and even having their sup-per at the office, generally complimentary catered gourmet. I have heard of some firms charging this meal to the client. Some of these firms even have beds or the like as the top brass feel that humans occasionally have to get some sleep. It allegedly increases their efficiency.

I usually got into the office around 9:30/10ish, leaving by 6 p.m. I would, however, enjoy a catered meal whenever I attended a Bar Association dinner. To boot, my firm picked up the tab. I just don't see how BigLaw could work their dinners into the client account:

- To research *Corporations Act*: .7 hours
- To draft partnership agreement: 3.75 hours
- To dine on baked Mediterranean sea bass while doing the above work: 1.25 hours (Lawyer had to eat slowly as there were lots of bones).

Nobody ever said access to justice was cheap.

What awestruck me is the sheer size of these firms, often occupying several floors. The lobby elevators in these skyscrapers often note that they stop on even- or odd-number floors. So to visit, you must know whether the lawyer is even or odd.

I practised for the most part in an 1800s virtual heritage house in suburban Toronto. It reminded me of the office of Atticus Finch. Not one client ever had to figure out which elevator to use.

I once attended to personally rush serve documents on a BigLaw lawyer. The receptionist (the 44th floor receptionist) made a call and out from the mailroom came a gentleman in a uniform. He had a name tag reading, "Mr. Beamish."

Soon, another gentleman wearing a similar uniform arrived and asked Mr. Beamish if everything was OK. This man's tag read "Mr. Wilson." I wondered whether my presence sparked an emergency situation requiring mailroom backup.

Mailrooms were a surprise. In my office, the mailroom was located on my assistant's desk. The mailman, Charlie, would arrive, say "Good morning, Angela," usually adding, "I hope some of these have cheques for Marcel."

I just can't imagine the downtown mailman riding up forty-four floors and saying, "Hey Beamish, I hope some of these envelopes contain cheques for McKenzie, MacDougall, and Sullivan. (Fictitious names of course. They are actually McKenzie, MacDougal, and Solomon).

But the large firms do have perks. I noticed a lady, also in a uniform, pushing a trolley carrying coffee, tea, and scrumptious-looking pastries. My office had something similar. Angela and I would take turns fetching those scrumptious pastries waiting in the nearby strip plaza at the Tim Hortons.

Another enviable perk is excellent tickets to sporting events. Unless you want to pay a scalper $200 for a $75 ticket for a Leafs hockey game, it is virtually impossible to secure a good seat. The large law firms hoard blocks of tickets to entertain clients. I actually scored a handful of gold seats at a Leafs game, all via a friendly BigLaw associate who had to forego the game as he suddenly had to stay late at the office. I never asked him what catered supper he had. I should have.

One problem at large firms is bureaucracy. A friend who worked at one (39th floor) wanted to rearrange his desk to face a window. He needed some committee approval; something like the "Furniture Motion Committee." They actually denied his application. He eventually quit the firm. Too bad. He was the guy who used to get me those hockey tickets.

Similar desk situations arose in my practice too. Fortunately, the requisite committee never once rejected my environmental plans. For years I enjoyed a great view of squirrels scooting up and down the decades-old maple tree in my front lawn.

Another feature of large firms is the specialized clientele they attract. I once visited one with a large base of mining-industry clients. The magazines in the reception area were not overly alluring to me. I did not expect the latest issue of *Mad Magazine*. However, I doubt most of us would have a tug of war over some publication like *The Mine and You*, or *News from Down Under*. And I for one would pass, however tempting, on an article called "7 Secrets about Zinc."

My office reception selection, in fact, had some humour magazines in the mix. I thought it would be a good idea to get clients laughing before I turned on the meter.

Initially my practice included a sizeable percentage of criminal-law work. There were not too many magazines out there catering specifically to these clients. I certainly never came across anything like *Your Guide to Canadian Prisons*.

I have no regrets in having missed out on practising in a BigLaw-type firm. I do think about those hockey tickets I was foregoing. But then again, given the years of the COVID-19 pandemic, the hardest hit were those ticket scalpers.

CHAPTER TEN

Lawyers, Lattés, and Other Delectables

"If this is coffee, please bring me some tea; but if
this is tea, please bring me some coffee."
~ Abraham Lincoln

There is more in the delivery of legal services these days than the traditional big-law, small-law, or even mid-law firms. How about restaurant law or box-store law? The past couple of decades have seen drastic changes in how and where legal services are provided. We now see law offices not only in traditional settings, such as tall buildings with elevators, but also in supermarkets, warehouse stores, and even cafés, as in the recently established Toronto café called "Lawyers and Lattés." (I'll have more to say about this one shortly.) Where is all of this heading?

I think about Atticus Finch, as played by Academy Award winner Gregory Peck in *To Kill a Mockingbird*. He practised out of his wooden veranda–equipped house in rural Alabama. Atticus Finch was a formidable lawyer—caring, attentive, and courageous. No elevator, but that was OK (like my office).

Fast forward a few decades. In the Toronto area one lawyer started changing the face of the law office by setting up several storefront branches in shopping malls. No appointment necessary. While you're out shopping for a new pair of Nikes, you can just drop in at the lawyer store and spill all the beans of your dysfunctional marriage to an attorney on duty. I suppose if you are charged with a serious crime, such as assault with a weapon, and you might want a lawyer who comes somewhat recommended, you may not take too much comfort in hearing someone tell you, "Just go to that office next to the Apple store at the Westmount Mall. Ask if the guy with the horn-rimmed glasses is in. He got me off on a speeding charge."

Not too long ago a law firm called Axess opened up several branches inside Walmart outlets in Ontario. This firm, like the mall lawyer's firm, has a fees menu stationed in front listing the cost of various services.

It occurred to me that clients might think they are just Walmart lawyers. I imagine that Walmart would be concerned about being dragged into potential malpractice litigation and accordingly they probably have stringent provisions in their leasing agreements to ensure that they distance themselves from the lawyers. It would not surprise me if they included conditions such as:

G: Independent Entity/i.e., you are not part of Walmart–NO WAY

14: Your lawyers will not wear yellow and blue smocks

15: Your fees list must be in round numbers; it cannot read something like, "Preparation of Will: $333"

16: You must not have a greeter at your entrance

17: Your clients must pay you directly at your office; they cannot use our self-checkout

These are simply my thoughts expressing my concern for Walmart's welfare.

Most recently, a lawyer in Toronto opened a café called "Lawyers & Lattés, where you can also get legal services. The café offers a fair array of food and drink. If a customer wants legal services, there are always a couple of lawyers on duty who will sit down at a table with the customer, now turned client. This person can opt for privacy away from, say, the college students sitting nearby with their Macs.

There is also a menu, or rather, fees list for legal services. I have not seen it, but even though it is an upscale café, I doubt it reads anything like "Wills: Basic: $250; Grande: $300; The Works: $500." Maybe they even have specials: "Try our combo: Pre-nupt and matrimonial home sale: $999." You never know. It could come in handy one day.

Their lawyer dress code is easy; they can show up in jeans no problem. The founder wishes to dispel lawyer stereotypes. He readily achieves this goal. I don't see Atticus Finch telling his client, "They have your fingerprints on the murder weapon. Looks serious. You can get the chair for this one. Can I get you a cappuccino?"

Actually, for more involved matters they partner with a network of lawyers whom they can call on. The principal jokingly refers to the concept as an "Uber for lawyers." I wonder if they will take that one a step further and indeed partner with Uber, networking with lawyers who also provide Uber transportation. This would be a super time saver. The client can get legal advice while, say, driving to the airport. Then again, the lawyer/operator would have to docket his or her time, reverting back to the taxi meter. The meter multiples of course would be units of "point 1." Just a thought.

I have not seen a law office open yet in one of my favourite stores, Costco. This is certainly food for thought. As for the food part, one aspect of Costco is the cluster of nosh stations where the roaming customer can stop for nibbles of cheese, cookies, or pickles. The servers usually slice the already small sample piece into several pieces, just to give you a taste. A tiny one.

I don't know what the law firm can offer parallel to these munchies; maybe a short soundbite of legal advice. Very short. A customer stops in front of a lawyer stranding behind a podium. The lawyer queries, "Your legal problem is?" The customer asks something simple like, "How do I get custody of my kids?" The lawyer responds, "Good question. Actually, our office is over there next to the tire centre. This week's special is divorces."

Another issue Costco would have to deal with is the fact that most of their products come in multiple quantities or giant sizes. A client might ask for a quote for the sale of his house and the lawyer may have to decline, saying, "Sorry. Can I interest you in selling three houses?" More food for thought.

A major boon about Costco shopping is their legendary satisfaction guarantee refund policy. This could be a problem with legal services. While customers have to line up at the refund counter for service, Costco might see itself getting letters from disgruntled clients from some penitentiary. "I'm not satisfied with my lawyer. I want a full refund now. I don't want to wait fourteen years. Receipt enclosed."

As I said, the face of the traditional law practice has been changing. I'm proudly old school. For me, lawyers such as Perry Mason and Atticus Finch are still my legal role models. I think, had these gentlemen been around today, they would indeed likely end up at Costco, but only to buy a jar of pickles. OK, maybe three jars.

CHAPTER ELEVEN

So Why Law? Kindergarten, Dresses, and Mistresses

"What hath night to do with sleep?"
~ John Milton, *Paradise Lost*

Or rather, what hath the law to do with justice, I ask. Give me justice, I say. But is the pursuit of justice why we become lawyers? We know all about getting clients and also getting rid of them (if need be and when possible). So why would one choose to become a lawyer?

My own voyage goes back to an indelible kindergarten incident. I actually went into this profession for the right reasons, and yes, it did actually have something to do with justice. While playing in the schoolyard I witnessed some kids swarming a classmate and snatching away his lunchbox. Almost instinctively I demanded that these bullies return it to the crying victim. In effect, I sought intervenor status, or the right to step up to the plate and offer my two cents worth. After listening to my eloquent and unassailable plea, the rogues grabbed my lunchbox too, knocking me to the ground. At least they granted me intervenor status.

Sitting there on the ground with tears in my eyes, I thought to myself, "This is not right." I wanted so much to right the wrongs. How? I cannot say that at age five I thought to myself, "That does it; when I grow up, I'm becoming a lawyer."

I did not even know what a lawyer was. After all, unlike doctors, most kids have little need for lawyers. Growing up, the most visible professional was the doctor. I even had a toy doctor's kit. It included a stethoscope, popsicle sticks, and even a vial of little colourful candies resembling M & Ms, which presumably represented drugs. They actually tasted good.

However, I have yet to see a toy lawyer's kit. What would that consist of? A podium? A barrister's wig? Maybe a bill? All unlikely bestsellers at Toys R Us.

My first meeting with a live lawyer was as a teenager when I accompanied my mother over a new fancy dress some dry cleaner had ruined. The lawyer told my mom we were going to "fix that cleaner." He asked her to leave the dress with him (exhibit 1, no doubt).

I was impressed by his confidence and demeanor and wished he would have been with me during that schoolyard lunchbox heist. The lawyer sent a fiery letter to that cleaning outfit demanding compensation, or else. The result? They ignored the admonition, and the case dissipated.

The lawyer's bill to my mother, incidentally, was $10. That looked like a princely sum to me, given that my allowance was a nickel a day. I recalled that run-in with that dentist whose lawyer also charged $10 for writing a letter and considering a life as a lawyer started to ferment in my brain.

However, the financial rewards of the law were not the prime ingredient in my pursuing a legal career. Ditto most lawyers. I never heard a colleague say, "Yep, the practice of law is a goldmine." We all have loftier reasons, no doubt. Surely we are more than mercenaries.

I will add that my mother never paid the $10. She reasoned she never recovered damages, so why pay. I guess this was also my first exposure to a unilaterally created contingency arrangement. She also never picked up that ruined dress. I wonder whether the lawyer regarded the dress as some form of compensation.

So why did I choose to go to law school? I knew I wanted to provide a valuable service, fixing wrongs. It came down to law or medicine, until that fateful day at Montreal's Expo 67. Expo, as it was known, was a world-class event that put Montreal on the map. It featured over one hundred pavilions with multinational scientific and entertainment exhibits.

After waiting in line under the hot sun for a while I entered the Health Pavilion where visitors would watch films of medical procedures. There were warnings posted that some of these scenes were not for the squeamish. In fact, every day a fair number of visitors fainted. They even actually employed university students, at about $2.50 per hour, who hovered around catching and reviving overly daring guests.

I went from room to room viewing different medical lectures and procedures and was quite fine—until the open-heart surgery clip. I recall a sudden odd sensation, like my ears being sucked into my head. As a student darted over to make the catch, I dropped, mumbling something eloquent like, "Ugggh." The path was now cleared for a career in law.

Actually, my fantasy calling then was to become a firefighter. These noble first responders always achieved a just result, from extinguishing a fire to extricating a cat from a tree. I recall high on my wish list was securing one of those cool firefighter hats.

But somehow my fantasy was not realized, and soon enough, there I was, my first day in law school. The dean assembled and welcomed the class. He quoted former U.S. Supreme Court Justice Story, who said, "The law is a jealous mistress, requiring long and constant courtship. It is not to be won by trifling favours but by lavish homage."

The point was, as lawyers we would have to spend many hours working. I never noticed how many hours Perry Mason worked. After all, in a fifty-two-minute episode there was only so much room to show him burning the midnight oil. No problem. I was in.

I was newly married at the time, and I told my wife about the dean's quote. Shoshana thought it was amusing, remarking that she did not mind our newly formed threesome.

However, the real world was not all courtroom drama. I initially worked for a general-practice firm. During my first week my boss sent me to the Land Registry office for a house closing with the vendor's lawyer. Although I did not expect a murder brief on day one, starting with a house closing was a downer. I just could not visualize Perry Mason meeting up with prosecutor Hamilton Burger at the Registry Office. Without ado, he hands Burger a cheque and Burger responds by giving him the house deed. Awesome! What a Netflix series that would make. Wow!

Where was the justice buzz? I thought to myself. Is this why I went to law school? I would very much have welcomed an "objection" from the vendor's lawyer. Even something like "You're not getting the house keys."

That evening when my good wife asked how my day went, I meekly confessed to the day's legal career highlight. She laughed and said, "I see you had some disenchantment with your mistress."

I thought about another quote, from that Dickens character Mr. Bumble, who said, "The law is an ass." I did, however, rationalize. After all, the legal profession is humbler than the medical one. Doctors call many diseases after the name of some pertinent physician. I am talking about conditions such as Alzheimer's, Crohn's, and even the undercooked chicken disease, salmonellosis. (Actually, the latter doctor was a vet, Dr. Daniel Elmer Salmon.)

Lawyers by contrast give the clients credit for the landmark cases, referring to their actual names, not the lawyers' names. These include the iconic cases like *Donoghue v. Stevenson* (negligence), or *Hadley v. Baxendale* (damages), *Miranda* (right to remain silent etc. on arrest); I have yet to see something like "Clarence Darrow's Case." We lawyers don't hog all the limelight.

However, the real world of lawyering did not always correspond to world-of-television law. I spent much of my student articling year at a commercial and real estate firm. Accompanying a senior lawyer to the registry office to watch him convey a house to the purchaser never made me jump and shout, "Another house deal has been closed. Justice is done. Yippee!"

This gets us to prestige: A factor in choosing law? I doubt it. The public's view of lawyers is often ambivalent. I once represented a person whose lawyer defrauded many clients. At the creditor's meeting with the lawyer's trustee in bankruptcy, one creditor asked whether the trustee was a lawyer. The trustee responded, "No, I'm an accountant." The creditor said, "Phew! That's a relief." Accountants one; lawyers zero.

Let me share the case that validated my choice of law. During my freshman practice year, an elderly gentleman, Morris, whose wife of many years died, retained me. The matrimonial home was registered in her name during her previous marriage. Morris, throughout the solid marriage, paid most of the expenses, including liquidating the mortgage. He was in his late seventies and now had special needs and limited funds.

Unfortunately, his wife in her will, signed shortly into their marriage, left everything to her son, who lived in Connecticut. The stepson/executor demanded that Morris forthwith vacate the home. We referred to him as, "The Connecticut Yankee."

I devoted most of my hours to this case, trying to make justice happen. Ultimately the trial judge ordered the Connecticut Yankee to pay a substantial sum from the estate to my client. The boost of morale was indescribable, and it rarely left me. The case was also my first reported case. Morris said to me, "Your greatness will start with this case." I'd like to say this prognostication was validated. But I will say there were other cases throughout that gave me that similar shot of satisfaction, leaving no doubt that I had chosen the right career.

What I took away from it all was that my presence on this planet counted. And I really didn't care that that case was not reported as "Strigberger's Case."

CHAPTER TWELVE

The Law: Real-World Style

"Education is what remains after one has forgotten what one has learned in school."
~ Albert Einstein

I s law-school learning always practical? Hmmm. I believe this genius's opinion describes the law-school experience bang on.

During our first week at McGill University's law school in Montreal, the librarian gave us a tour of the law-school library. As our small group meandered through the labyrinth of shelves of volumes of law reports, many stemming from the 19th century, suddenly I heard a "pssst." I looked over and a gentleman, who introduced himself as Duncan, a graduate student from England, started to chat with me. He said, "Henceforth, as a man of justice, you will never view life's events from the perspective lay people do." It felt spooky. Was this a blessing or a curse? This was also the first time I ever heard the word "henceforth."

I remember our first tort class. We studied an 1800s British case called *Winterbottom v. Wright*. Winterbottom was a postal service employee and due to Wright's faulty repair of the coach, he suffered an injury. He sued Wright but lost as the court ruled there was no privity of contract between him and the repairman. Therefore, Wright owed no duty to Winterbottom. Badda boom badda bing. (The latter are my judicial words.)

At the end of the class, I was proud of my newly acquired knowledge, knowing I was on my way to becoming a lawyer. That evening I shared my progress with my father, relating this case to him, who, incidentally, was helping me with the funding of my tuition, books, and such. Eyebrows raised, he said, "Is that all you learned today? Those horse-drawn coaches are dangerous to start with. Anyway, these days trucks deliver the mail. Why waste time studying this useless case?" I certainly did not view it from this perspective.

Shortly afterwards we came across the iconic 1700s property case of *Armory v. Delamirie*, where a chimney sweep, Armory, found a piece of jewellery, a ring. He took it for appraisal to the jeweller Delamirie, who kept it for a while and then refused to return the stones. Armory sued. The court held for the plaintiff noting that finders' rights are paramount to all, other than the rightful owner. In effect, possession is nine points of the law.

I was exuberant with my knowledge of property law. I told my dad. He took a puff of his cigarette and said, "This is what they teach you in law school? That's obvious. That chimney sweep was stupid. He should never have left the ring out of his sight. Some jewellers are crooks." He did have a point, though I no longer viewed it this way. I did breathe a sigh of relief given that he did not suggest reconsidering his financial assistance trajectory.

We soon studied the seminal 1928 negligence case of *Donoghue v. Stevenson*, where the plaintiff at a café in Scotland noticed a decomposed snail in her pale-coloured ginger beer after pouring it out of an opaque bottle into a tumbler. She became ill and successfully sued the manufacturer. The court affirmed that negligence is a tort, and that the manufacturer owed a duty of care to its potential consumers.

This case was huge, but I felt uneasy and decided not to share it with my dad. I did not want to risk disrupting my funding chain. My father, however, sensed my anxiety and asked me what I had learned today. I quickly gave him a short case summary. He said, "Interesting. That lady would never even have seen that snail had she been drinking Pepsi." My dad's kind funding assistance continued uninterrupted.

But does this exciting academic inculcation prepare us sufficiently for practice in the real world? The next stage after law school was articling at a law firm. I was interviewed by a seasoned trial lawyer, Hank. I proudly handed him my law-school transcript, showing great grades, the highest being an A in admiralty law. Hank chuckled and said, "Next time two ships collide at the intersection of Queen Street and Bay Street in downtown Toronto, you'll be the first I'll call." He ripped the transcript in two. I was taken aback. I felt as though my legal career had just sailed into the Bermuda Triangle. I suddenly had empathy for Winterbottom.

Hank continued. "Forget about what they taught you in law school. The real world of justice is monumentally different. You'll learn that quickly. Welcome to the firm."

Hank continued telling me it's all about reading people, knowing what makes them tick, and showing respect and exercising civility. He noted, "When you go to the courthouse to file a document, there will always be a clerk with a bushy moustache who will give you a tough time and impulsively reject it. As well, there will be some kind woman with a ponytail who will bend over backwards to accept it. It won't help if you tell either of them that you earned an A in admiralty."

I recall my first couple of courthouse attendances to file documents. I looked around carefully, but I never spotted either the guy with the bushy moustache or the lady with the ponytail. But I quickly learned whom to approach or avoid.

Throughout the year, Hank kept on stressing this theme. He would say, "Above all, know your judges. Believe it or not, they're human, like us." This lesson was invaluable. However, during my early days in practice, I did not always follow Hank's advice. Once I pled a client guilty to a charge of automobile joyriding. Given the client's previous clean record and young age I expected him to get a suspended sentence or a small fine. To my surprise, the judge hit him with ninety days in the slammer.

Dejected, I called Hank about advice regarding appeal. After mentioning the judge's name, he laughed and said, "Didn't you know about a year ago some fool took off with Judge Graham's new Corvette, wrecking it beyond repair? What you did is you brought the little piggy to the wolf." Thereafter I virtually always meticulously researched my judges.

I later had a guilty plea in a drunk-driving matter. It was the client's second offence, and this usually called for some jail time. Our judge was a former navy vice admiral. I learned he had a soft spot for sailors and things oceanic. By chance, my client was born in Halifax, Nova Scotia. I just knew I had to appeal to the judge's instincts for justice (the pertinent ones of course).

If only I could say something like, "My client is a former midshipman. His joy is to sail the seven seas. He loves reading and his favourite novel is *Moby Dick*." If only. But alas! My submissions to sentence went something like, "Billy was born in Halifax. He came to central Canada looking for a better future. He would like to soon visit his parents, who still live on the east coast. He is remorseful for his misdeed."

The judge listened attentively. As he pondered sentence disposition, I wondered how much further I could push the justice envelope. I resisted the temptation to step forward and dance a quick hornpipe. To my surprise, the judge said, "This is a serious matter. However, given all the circumstances, the court will give the Maritimer a break." After a stern rebuke, he hit him with only a high fine. I certainly did not credit my successful result to my A in admiralty.

I told Hank about the case, and he gave me a thumbs up. I then related the case to my father, mentioning Hank's wise advice about knowing your judges. He said to me, "That's obvious. Didn't they teach you all that in law school?"

Now do we all agree that Einstein was right about law school education? What don't they teach you in law school? Here's a magic bullet: How to be persuasive.

CHAPTER THIRTEEN

Successful Law Practice: The Magic Bullet

"All you need in this life is *ignorance and con-fidence*, and then success is sure."

~ *Mark Twain*

I s this the magic bullet to practising law successfully? OK, so he wasn't focusing on the legal profession. Nonetheless, the confidence part is understandable. The ignorance, maybe.

As lawyers we have to be persuasive. For this it helps to be observant and to attain and use certain information, or to know when not to use it. I found it all boils down to understanding and appreciating the human element. Those you have to persuade have to like you and/or your case. Or as Tweedledee in *Through the Looking Glass* said, "contrariwise." They have to dislike the other side or their case. (My Tweedledee quote is confined only to the "contrariwise.")

And all of us, be we judges, jury members, or clients, have quirks that govern our likes and dislikes. And to ascertain these quirks, it helps to notice other's reactions and assess which way the wind is blowing.

I recall once being in a motions court. The judge seemed impatient, periodically interrupting counsel saying, "Your argument is not enlightening me." This concerned me as I waited to be called. I thought initially my chances of success were about 30/70. Given the judge's apparent mood my confidence level plummeted a bit. So did my assessment.

My opponent, more seasoned than I, was dressed to kill, wearing a fancy three-piece suit and sporting a gold chain pocket watch in his vest. He reminded me of barrister Sir Wilfred Robarts, portrayed by Charles Laughton in the iconic film *Witness for the Prosecution*. He rose to argue first, frequently looking at his pocket watch. He sounded smug, suggesting my opposition to his motion was a complete waste of the court's time. The judge did not interrupt him at all. Uh oh! He did however fidget uncomfortably whenever "Sir Wilfred" touched his pocket watch or even his vest.

My turn came. I took a risk, opening with, "Your Honour, I trust you will find my argument enlightening." The judge emitted a quick smile and said, "Proceed sir." He eagerly lifted his pen to make notes. I did not know what to make of it. I did not dare sneak a gaze at my wristwatch. Fortunately, his ruling was favourable. Did he like my case? My opening quip? Or just maybe he did not like the other lawyer's gold pocket watch. I'll never know. But he must have liked (or disliked) something that enlightened him.

I recall another case soon after getting called to the Bar where I attended traffic court representing a client on a minor offence. It was raining. Once in the courtroom, I didn't know I had to take off my light-coloured trench coat. When my case was called, the Justice of the Peace discretely hinted to me about removing my trench coat saying, "It's not raining in here, Columbo." I apologized and took it off. After a short trial, the J. P. said to me, "Summation Lieutenant?"

The charge was dismissed. I didn't think my argument was that great. And my confidence was a bit rattled. Was success aided by my ignorance? Or maybe the judge just liked Columbo? Something persuaded him.

I was not that successful in another trial where I wanted to argue an evidentiary point just before the lunch break. I confidentially said to the judge, quoting Shakespeare, "I'll be quick. 'Brevity is the soul of wit.'" The judge responded, quoting French humorist Rabelais, "OK sir but remember, 'An empty belly has no ears.'" To this day I regret going with Shakespeare over Rabelais. My ignorance here did not achieve success.

And can candor and honesty sometimes hurt? Whenever I would interview a client in a personal-injury case, they would ask me how long this case would take? (This question followed "how much will I get," followed by the terser, "how much will you get?")

As these cases can take years to resolve, I would point to a tall old maple outside my suburban two-story office and say something like, "Before this case is done, those leaves will change colours, then fall off, then the branches will be snow covered, and then the leaves will grow back. This cycle will repeat."

Not long after this spiel in a potentially lucrative case, the client bolted, switching to a high-rise downtown office lawyer. I asked my successor why the client jumped ship. He told me I had left him with the impression his case will drag on forever. The client especially did not like my story about that tree. This explanation upset me. It was the truth. At least he did not file a disciplinary complaint with the Law Society alleging something like, my lawyer is callous and cold-blooded. He compared my case to a pile of leaves.

And so, what does it take to persuade successfully? We all know about methods such as do not overreach, keep it simple, and use stories and analogies. All true though here I struck out with that analogy of that maple.

We have to realize we are constantly being judged by what we say or do or, at times contrariwise, what we do not say or do. Aristotle said, "Wisdom is the reward you get for a lifetime of listening when you would rather have talked." No doubt he meant listening and observing. But does it not all come down to having a sense of the human element? One more thing. Did I persuade you? Or at least influence you? Why don't we look into our influencers a bit more?

CHAPTER FOURTEEN

Influencers: Birds, Bees, and Even Lawyers Have Them

"I feel a very unusual sensation—if it is not indigestion, I think it must be gratitude."

~ Benjamin Disraeli

Who were your influencers? I am talking people whose ideas or conduct shaped some major paths you took. As I am sipping a green tea and looking out my study window, I see a gentleman walking his beagle. He looks just like Ted (the gentleman, not the beagle). And who is Ted you ask?

Ted was a top-notch Crown Attorney (aka District Attorney to our neighbours to the south) before I got called to the Bar. I sometimes snuck off from my articling job to sit in his Superior Court courtroom, mesmerized, watching him prosecute high-profile murder cases. Ted was brilliant and relentless, regularly securing convictions. My goal was to practise criminal law. I admired the man but dreaded ever coming up against him.

About a month into practice, I landed a minor $200 damage, parking lot hit-and-run charge. The client pleaded ignorance, saying he did not even hear a bang. As this was my first trial, I believed him implicitly.

I spent ages on preparation, including research in the courthouse Great Library. There was no Google then to query something like, "Client hits car, no boom, innocent? Please?"

We rehearsed intensely for the big day, repeatedly going over the anticipated cross-examination. Trial day arrived and I was a bundle of nerves. As I entered the then Provincial Court courtroom, my jaw dropped. Who was the prosecutor? Ted of course. I thought what was he doing in this minor-league forum? My client was hardly a serial killer. I did not think Ted was here to watch me in action, returning the compliment.

Ted vetted his docket list and he asked me how we intended to plead. With zero thinking but 100% passion, I blurted out, "Not guilty. This is about justice." Ted smiled. I imagined General Santa Anna had a similar smile after Lieutenant Colonel William Travis notified him that he was not surrendering the Alamo.

My client testified. To my surprise, when the judge asked the prosecution, "Cross-examination?" Ted replied, "No questions." Nor did Ted offer any summation following my fervent argument, readily rivalling Clarence Darrow's closing address in *Leopold and Loeb*. The judge found a reasonable doubt and acquitted my client. Ted came over and shook my hand, saying, "Great job, Marcel."

I never figured out what Ted was doing that day on a Mickey Mouse case, nor why he did not unload on me. I knew Ted's comment was sincere. (After all, my presentation was awesome!) But this case inspired me over my forty years of practice, charging me with moxie in precarious litigation situations. Ted was an influencer. Thanx Ted.

Then there was Hank, my articling principal and mentor. One night after a reception and about to take the bus home, Hank offered me a lift to the bus stop. When we got there, he drove by and took me all the way home,

driving well out of his way. I asked why and he said, "When you start practising, remember this: Always give your clients more than you promise."

These words resonated with me, and they became part of my mission statement. I will admit now that when I would sneak off to court to
watch Ted, it was actually while working for Hank. I soon developed guilt
pangs, reminiscent of Dostoevsky's iconic *Crime and Punishment* character, Rodion Raskolnikov. It bugged me. Do I confess or not?

I did come clean with Hank. He laughed and said, "You'll learn a lot
observing these trials. I used to do it too. That is what being a law student
is all about." His magnanimous reaction reminded me of that scene in *Les
Misérables* where when the police showed up after nabbing Jean Valjean
with one of the bishop's silver candlesticks, the bishop tells them it was a
gift and that he neglected to give Jean Valjean the second matching one.
Hank was an influencer. Thanx Hank.

Then there was Eugene, a current guru in persuasive legal writing.
His wisdom included tidbits such as keeping it simple, clear, and focused.
In a document, say up front what relief you are seeking. Don't write it like
a mystery novel. Avoid fancy verbose fillers. Instead of "at that point in
time" say "then." Instead of "until such time as," say "until." My favourite is,
"Bottom line, good legal writing looks as if someone other than a lawyer
has written it."

He generously shares this wisdom with the profession. I found it
insightful to remember judges are really human, inundated with documents, and that they actually appreciate reading lawyer stuff where they
can say to themselves, "For a change, this looks like it was drafted by
someone standing in line with me at Starbucks. Eugene was an influencer.
Thanx Eugene.

I fondly reminisce about my influencers. We all have some. Take
a moment to think about them and thank them. It goes well with that
green tea.

CHAPTER FIFTEEN

Avoiding Trouble—No Problem

"Intellectuals solve problems. Geniuses prevent them."
~ Albert Einstein

With respect to geniuses, I am not sure Einstein had lawyers in mind.

Do lawyers ever experience trouble or create problems? Unlikely. But just in case they do, can they do something to prevent same? I recall my first day as an articling student. My principal, Hank, sent me to the land registry office to close a house deal with a lawyer, a "Mr. Buckley," much my senior. This involved handing him a deed and keys in exchange for a certified cheque. As I proceeded with trepidation, Mr. Buckley, sensing my anxiety, remarked, "As a lawyer you always have to be tough. Take no prisoners." This comment took me aback. What was I supposed to do here and now to act tough? Throw the keys out the window?

I related that chat to Hank, and he said, "Remember, in our profession one party might make war on another party. Do not make war on the other lawyer." Fortunately, I followed Hank's sage advice and I developed some routines to deal with problems and troubles, some of which I wish to share (the routines, not the troubles).

Firstly, I found it useful to keep my ego at the door. It was OK to blink first, especially in family domestic cases where the emotional temperature can rise quickly. Often clients would attend with letters from their spouse's lawyer, spouting vitriol, reading something like, "My client will not condone your monstrous acts."

I would not hesitate to call the other lawyer and introduce myself as representing that resident of Loch Ness. It broke the ice. Often the case concluded with a speedy resolution, saving the clients big-time money and us avoidable aggravation.

I never regretted blinking first. Digressing slightly, likely my most important first blink was my marriage proposal. I made my pitch to Shoshana while inside the Humour Pavilion at Montreal's exhibition, "Man and His World." I figured had she said "no," I would have responded with, "Only kidding. This is the Humour Pavilion." True, I did have that safety net for my ego. But it turned out to be a worthwhile blink.

As well, if you do mess up, apologize. It will not diminish your toughness. Never mind Mr. Buckley. Mark Twain said it best: "Always acknowledge a fault. This will throw those in authority off their guard and give you an opportunity to commit more."

I recall once participating in a nasty family-law mediation where the opposing lawyer called my client a "contemptible cretin." While I pondered my response, my client said to me, "Marcel, don't go there. Rise above all that."

Somewhat rattled, I asked the other lawyer to step out, and I said, "Surely, Harold, counsel of your ilk is capable of better than that." Harold reflected for a minute, returned, and apologized. My client and I both felt vindicated.

If you are wrong, own up to it. (Fortunately, Harold did not exercise Mark Twain's suggested opportunity to "commit more.")

More about apologies. A mere explanation is not an apology. We were on a cruise once on the second-level deck when our sleep was interrupted by a little clanging noise. Actually, it sounded more like our bed was lodged inside Notre Dame Cathedral's twelve-ton bell. I complained to guest relations and the "guest relater" confidently calmly explained, saying something like, "Oh yes, that's the fourth ballast cadiddle buttressing the intermediate engine on the port side."

"Of course," I said, "That's helpful. Now at least I'll know why I won't be getting a wink of sleep on this cruise. Thanx."

Don't just rationalize it. Fix it.

And speaking of machines going wrong, this brings me to my major pet peeve, technology. Though I appreciate its value, I am a technophobe loathing our total dependence on it. I won't say I'm a Luddite; however, if I were living in Salem Massachusetts, I would circulate a petition to go after Siri.

I am now a boomer, happily retired from law practice. But while in practice I noticed several common problems, especially relating to emails. Firstly, lawyers often feel compelled to respond instantly. And too often, after cooling off, they regret doing so. The "undo" feature lasts for only seconds. It would be nice if these replies could contain a caveat saying something like, "I reserve the right to recant that anatomical reference." Alas, this feature is not yet available.

Another problem is recipient error. A colleague once meant to address an email in an emotionally charged divorce matter to his client Marcus. After keying in "Marc" his system sent it to "Marcel," aka yours truly. It contained sensitive property and custody recommendations. I called him, admonishing that he be more careful, adding that I would not give up custody as he suggested, of the family beagle, Bentley. (I don't know if he heeded my advice.)

And most important in our quest to avoid trouble is to maintain our sense of humour. We all have one. To paraphrase Stephen Leacock, we just have to kindly observe the incongruities of life. You need not be a Seinfeld, or attack anybody, or tell jokes. For example, I once dealt with a fax-obsessed lawyer. Our office received multiple faxes from him almost daily. We referred to him as Dr. Fax. Whenever we heard the fax whirring, our staff would chuckle saying, "Must be Dr. Fax doing another office call." Or "What is he prescribing now?" One day there were no faxes from him. My assistant said, "The good doctor must be out golfing."

This playful attitude cleared the air, boosted morale, and helped avoid undue tension. However, nothing works all of the time to prevent trouble. Einstein aside, I also respect another renowned philosopher, Yogi Berra. He noted, "The other teams could make trouble for us if they win." Still, I hope some of my thoughts about preventing unnecessary hassles have been helpful. Does achievement of this goal make a sensible resolution? No problem.

CHAPTER SIXTEEN

Mistakes, Errors, and Omissions—
in Legalese: Boo-Boos

"I never made a mistake in my life. I thought I did once, but I was wrong."
~ Charles M. Schulz, creator of the comic strip *Peanuts*

A s careful as we are to avoid problems, do lawyers still blunder? What is a mistake? When I think of historical mistakes, I visualize the Leaning Tower of Pisa. What happened? Surely the architect should have noticed that it was not rising according to plan. None of us would allow our houses to be built off perpendicular like that without at least emailing the builder saying, "I don't know. Looks a bit slanted to me. When you get a chance, please drop by and have a peek."

I Googled to see if anybody ever took legal action but saw nothing even remotely resembling *Municipality of Pisa v. the Tower Professionals*.

My own recollection of the mistake concept goes back to when I was ten years old and I accidentally dropped my younger brother while playfully performing an over-the-shoulder wrestling airplane spin. This aerodynamic manoeuvre gone wrong did not sit well with my dad. He was not consoled by my eloquent pleas that it was just an accident. I won't go into details of the punishment outcome other than say I should have been offered a cigarette and a blindfold.

Which brings me to negligence and the circa 1932 game-changer landmark case of *Donoghue v. Stevenson*. In short, May Donoghue suffered physical injury and nervous shock after finding a decomposed snail in her ginger beer while in a pub. Totally understandable. She sued the manufacturer, Stevenson, and her claim was successful even though there was no privity of contract between her and the manufacturer. The court delivered access to justice, ruling that the manufacturer owed a duty of care not to harm its neighbour. Most likely this ruling acted as a deterrent to others not to be sloppy as I have never come across another case of a decomposed snail in a bottle of ginger beer in a pub.

However, negligence is not generally strict. If there is anything any law student remembers from law school, it's two words: "reasonably" and "foreseeable." In trying to determine negligence, the iconic phrase is whether the tortfeasor acted like the "reasonable man on the Clapham omnibus." (I would have preferred law schools here to say something more local, perhaps like the "Toronto subway.")

This hypothetical person is supposed to be your Mr. Average. He is not overly cautious, yet he is prudent enough to go out after a bout of freezing rain and dump a shovel of salt on his frosty walk so that reasonable people visiting him later on don't slip and fall and break a reasonable leg.

The question is what he (or she) would have done under the circumstances. But it is not always easy to admit screwing up. I often heard clients involved in motor-vehicle accidents plead, "I looked both ways before entering the intersection. The coast was clear and suddenly, bang, this guy came out of nowhere."

I usually asked innocently, "But surely he had to come out of somewhere?"

"No, he wasn't there when I looked. I tell you he just came out of nowhere," he replied with the innocence of Forrest Gump.

As I experienced a number of similar rationalizations over the years, I wondered, is there a "nowhere"? I gave this matter some thought. I looked in a dictionary, and it defined nowhere as "a place that does not exist." At least there is an element of certainty in that definition.

And how do we react when we drop the ball? I once arrived at a court hearing at 9:55 thinking the start time was 10:00. The judge bellowed that it was scheduled for 9:00. I responded with, "I'm sorry sir." He was not too forgiving, saying, "An apology is just a social crutch." Fortunately, after raking me over the coals first, he adjourned my hearing. I was thinking about what else I could have told him to express my regret. I doubt it would have helped to say, "It was an honest mistake," or "oops," or "I was caught in traffic." It certainly would not have been wise to say, "Make no mistake about it. I thought I was five minutes early."

We lawyers carry mandatory Errors and Omissions insurance, aka E and O insurance. For some reason, that term reminds me of a Monopoly game railroad. But the price is a lot higher than $50 if you ever land here. Six thousand dollars deductible plus additional annual penalties. I'd rather take a ride on that Clapham omnibus (or make it that Toronto subway).

Now here's a surprise. Even judges make mistakes. Our Notices of Appeal read something like this:

1. The learned trial judge erred in that he …

2. The learned trial judge also erred in that he …

3. The learned trial judge further erred in that he …

Judges are human. I don't know about you, but after this appeal, I'd hate to plead another case before this learned trial judge.

We all make mistakes sooner or later. I am reminiscing. Had I known as a kid what I know now, I wonder if I could have gotten off free had I told my dad that my airplane spin with my brother would have been approved by that gentleman on the Clapham Street omnibus.

Now that we have established that lawyers are indeed human and make mistakes, and get into trouble, are all lawyers happy with their choice of career? Uh huh!

CHAPTER SEVENTEEN

The Unhappy Lawyer: It's Not About the Journey

"Happiness depends upon ourselves."

~ Aristotle

I guess like Shakespeare, Aristotle also never practised law. Hey lawyers! Is everybody happy? If you're happy and you know it clap your hands. You may be one of the lucky ones. Many of our colleagues are not exactly thrilled practising law. As Nanki-Poo the prince in Gilbert and Sullivan's *The Mikado* might say, the best way they could express their joys of law practice would be "modified rapture."

I Googled "unhappy lawyers" and my search showed 17,200,000 results. There are sights entitled "I hate being a lawyer," "Why lawyers are unhappy," and "7 reasons why lawyers are unhappy." One comment even read, "Practice of law is the opposite of sex. Even when it's good, it's lousy." I'm glad I did not conduct this research during my pre-retirement days. Then again, when I got called to the Bar of Ontario in the mid-1970s there was no Google. No computers in law offices. This meant no emails or texts to hound you wherever you went—at the office or away. In fact, one major cause of stress mentioned is technology, including the speed at which it changes.

Our work at that time seemed less rushed. We would get a nasty letter in the mail from some colleague who in his previous life was no doubt a cross between a pit bull and Captain Bligh. We would mull over it and leisurely dictate a reply—after taking his name in vain of course. We would then read the draft letter, having cooled off by now, and mail out a more civil and effective response, leaving out what we thought of the opponent or his client, or where they can go.

And of course, when we left the office, there were no emails or texts following our departure home. This type of distraction perhaps can affect one's work/life balance. My being a technophobe, it had its advantages. I moved very slowly in the tech advance lanes. I was even suspicious of the stickie note.

And naturally, when lawyers are expected to respond to electronic communications instantly, we find ourselves working more hours. The long hours are another major cause of dissatisfaction with our work. This problem is especially prevalent in Biglaw firms, where associates push themselves hard, hoping to become partners. But once they achieve this status, are they happy? One lawyer who reached this goal did not think so, saying, "Being a partner means I have a bigger share of the pie. And where does this leave me? With more pie."

Another issue for lawyer dissatisfaction is a common stigma, namely that lawyers are shysters, long winded, and greedy ambulance chasers. Even when the public says something positive about our profession, the inference can sound negative. For example, there is a bar/restaurant in my community called "Honest Lawyer Restaurant." I never read the menu. I wouldn't trust it.

On a recent trip to the U.S. during the pandemic, the customs officer asked me to remove my mask so he could get a good look at my face. I joked with him, suggesting I was a member of an honourable profession, saying, "Would it help to tell you I am a lawyer?" He replied, "Actually, this might make it worse."

And what do many lawyers do about the problem? They leave the profession of course, going into other callings. Way other in some cases. I had a lawyer friend who became a baker, owning his own shop. I was curious about how he was doing hour-wise, and I remarked that surely he must rise early to bake those goodies. He told me he considered his products his friends. He took pride in his creations and his customers regularly showered him with praise. We chatted, and he reminded me that to our knowledge there was never anything disparaging said in the literature about bakers. Shakespeare never said, "First let's kill all the bakers." Not surprisingly, when I asked him, he said yes, that he often gives his customers a "Baker's dozen," throwing in an extra bagel.

Lawyers never get that credit. Then again to be fair, it's not like we can replicate a similar gesture of magnanimity. What can we do? Add a thirteenth juror?

I think about why I went into the legal profession. I always had the urge to let right prevail. This urge was also nurtured by one of my fictional heroes, Perry Mason, who would generally expose the real killer, who was usually stupid enough to be sitting in the courtroom.

I was a bit disillusioned once I started practising as most of my practice consisted of civil litigation and family-law cases. I did some criminal work but the majority of these cases could be classified summary conviction offenses or misdemeanors. I never once cross-examined a prosecution witness only to have him blurt out, "OK, OK. You got me. Your client is innocent. I shoplifted that toothbrush."

Here's a possible career switch. Oscar Mayer, the meat giant, has the call out for applications for drivers of its Wienermobiles. These are 27-foot-long hot dogs on wheels that travel all over touting the Oscar Mayer Wiener brand. It is apparently a coveted position for which there are oodles of applicants of which only twelve or so are chosen. They are called "Hotdoggers." (You cannot say Oscar Mayer is not imaginative.)

The lucky candidates get trained at a facility called "Hot Dog High." A spokesperson noted that given the competition, one has a better chance of getting admitted into an Ivy League university. One sight described this position as "the best job ever."

Any lawyers considering a career switch? I have run across plenty of colleagues who were disillusioned with the practice of law. Given that much of the glamour of lawyers is questionable, I can see this position as being of interest to many of counsel.

Apparently, these Hotdoggers are mini-celebrities. They pull into some town with their Wienermobile, where they participate in media and social events, and they get greeted by oodles of screaming fans.

In all my time as a working lawyer, I for one never got greeted by anyone when I used to pull up in my Camry at the local courthouse. (Actually, I would occasionally get greeted by someone screaming at me over a much-coveted parking spot.)

Even Shakespeare might have had good things to say about the OMW position. I can't imagine the bard saying, "First, let's kill all the Hotdoggers."

I can, however, see a number of legal issues or situations arising out of this job. Firstly, there is the Wienermobile itself. What if there's an accident? There are many legal cases on insurance coverage revolving about whether a certain vehicle is an automobile. I can easily foresee some insurance company arguing that it is not as there is nothing in the *Insurance Act* stating that insurance coverage is mandatory for a mammoth sausage.

I also see employment issues. At Hot Dog High, the lucky candidates will be taught numerous hot-dog puns and slogans, like "cut the mustard," which they'll have to utter in front of their hot-dog craving audiences all over. Sooner or later, I can see some of these guys cracking under the stress of having to constantly sing, "Oh I wish I was an Oscar Mayer wiener."

The good thing is, in the event of a road accident, it is most unlikely the operator would hit and expect to remain anonymous and take off. It is certainly unlikely a police officer arriving at the scene would bother asking the victim, "Did you get his licence number?" Uhh, officer.

My above discussion is accurate other than I recently found out that in 2023 Oscar Mayer is making a couple of changes to the iconic vehicle, changing its name from Weinermobile to Frankmobile. And the Hotdoggers will now be known as "Frankfurters." This is the first such name change in eighty-seven years. And I thought lawyers were conservative.

I also came across another occupation that may be of interest to disgruntled lawyers considering a career change. How about a gondolier in Venice? My wife and I visited Venice not long ago. It was a fine summer evening, and we decided to do what comes naturally in this charming city, namely, take a gondola ride. I asked the gondolier how much. The Venetian air was charged with romance and passion, and price, of course, was of no concern. The good fellow replied, "€150 per hour, sir." (About 225 Canadian loonies.) I said, "Thank you, sir," and we decided instead to settle for a chocolate gelato. This also comes naturally.

While strolling along San Marco Square consuming our gelati, Shoshana and I discussed the gondolier's charging €150 per hour. Many lawyers would only wish to make this much, or almost double what Legal Aid pays per hour. I asked myself why should a gondolier charge more than a lawyer? What do they have that we don't have? I decided to make a comparison.

First, I considered the popularity factor.

People generally have fantasies about gondoliers being romantic minstrels who sing as they wind their way through the canals. A ride along Venice's labyrinth of waterways can often be a fairy-tale experience.

A visit to a lawyer evokes a slightly different atmosphere. The greatest similarity to the aforementioned experience one can draw is that many clients claim that lawyers have taken them for a ride. I don't know about the singing part, but I'm sure that if you ask an assessment officer reviewing a lawyer's bill, none will tell you that clients have ever suggested that their lawyer, while conducting a cross-examination of a witness, breaks out singing "O Sole Mio." Lawyers, however, are known for singing the blues.

As for the romantic part, there are some lawyers whose love lives would leave even the most colourful gondolieri drifting far behind on the Grand Canal. But this reflection is not about Bill Clinton.

And lawyers and gondoliers are both popularized prominently in the arts. Gilbert and Sullivan wrote an operetta called *The Gondoliers* about the enchanting life on Venice's canals. Then again, William Shakespeare wrote, "Let's kill all the you-know-whats."

Then there is responsibility. If lawyers mess up, it's likely the client will sue them. The gondolier's job is relatively claim free, short of his running his gondola into another, at all of five kilometres per hour. However, gondoliers probably do have some form or errors-and-omissions insurance. You never know when some disgruntled client might turn around and sue the gondolier for screwing up the song *Funiculi, Funicula*.

Then there is training. I found that although lawyers invest years as students, we constantly had to pursue professional development. A gondolier can remain at his comfort level indefinitely. After all, what is left after the teacher shows you how to stand upright in the back of the gondola and push your oar? I don't imagine there was a newsflash in the Gondolier's Newsletter recently that proclaimed: "Gondolieri! Those black-and-white striped shirts you have been wearing since the year 1542 are no longer valid after October 1. After that date you must switch to sleeveless white undershirts."

And perhaps the best part of the job as compared with lawyers is that all gondoliers get paid in cash immediately. Over the barrel. Or should I say, over the paddle? After Lorenzo says "arrivederci" to you, he has already pocketed your €150. With lawyers, in most cases, unless they get all their money up front, they can calmly say arrivederci to their fee. They will have a receivable that will be as useful as an umbrella in Pompeii the day Vesuvius erupted. However, this may sometimes still be better than a government-issued Legal Aid certificate.

A trip to Venice can certainly entice lawyers to make a career change. So, what are lawyers waiting for? They have choices. Anybody know where you can get a good deal on those striped shirts?

So how do I feel about having spent decades as a practising lawyer? Charles Dickens comes to mind, where he says, "It was the best of times, it was the worst of times, it was the spring of hope, it was the winter of despair, things were great, things were lousy." OK, Dickens didn't quite say that latter couplet. But isn't that the way it is for most of us? It helped greatly that I worked in a small firm; I was a sole practitioner. I always strove to do the right thing. I promptly returned messages, I always treated people with respect, and I never lost my cool. OK, as Captain Corcoran of *H.M.S. Pinafore* might say, "hardly ever."

And so, is the lawyer's journey that gloomy? As any lawyer might say or should say, "yes and no." Read on.

CHAPTER EIGHTEEN

Lawyers—the Good: The Journey Is Not That Gloomy

"Lawyers are like professional wrestlers. They pretend to get
mad and fight, but then they socialize after a trial is over."
~ Robert Whitlow

The legal profession. All good? Then again, Shakespeare said, "First,
let's kill all the lawyers." One thing for sure, I would not have taken
him on as a client.

I retired about five years ago after over forty years in the trenches.
Let me share some thoughts on what is good about our profession. Firstly,
there is camaraderie among lawyers, even extending to soon-to-be lawyers. I worked my way through McGill law school as a Montreal tour guide
for Gray Line Sightseeing. While passing the courthouse I would announce
I was a law student. Invariably my guests often included lawyers. Some
would offer me encouraging comments such as, "You will be in for quite
an experience." One lawyer from St. Louis handed me his business card
saying if I'm ever in St. Louis to give him a call. I still have his card after
about fifty years. You never know. Renewing our ties is on my bucket list.
This invitation adds another dimension to the title "Meet Me in St. Louis."

The lawyers were also my best tippers. I wondered whether this professional courtesy applied to other callings. I recall guiding a group of undertakers. I was tempted to blurt out something like, "I am working my way through the Collège de Québec des Mortuaires." I resisted this temptation. (Actually, there is no such collège.) However, I often wonder how generously undertakers tip their own.

Fortunately, our camaraderie is present even during litigation. Shakespeare also said, "Do as adversaries in law, strive mightily but eat and drink as friends." (Presumably before they kill us.)

I once had an opponent colleague invite me for lunch during a trial break. My client, originally from Hungary, was taken aback, saying in Hungary opposing lawyers would never socialize. True or anecdotal? I never checked it out further by Googling something like "Hungarian lawyers/trial/lunch practices."

However, to ease my client's concerns, I took a rain cheque on that lunch. I did not think it helpful to tell him what Shakespeare said about eating and drinking as friends. He might then have reminded me about Shakespeare's other comment about lawyers.

Another quality we practise is empathy. A colleague once called me saying I had misadvised a former client and he was going to sue me. Expressing the professional empathy I expected, he said, "We'll issue our claim soon. However, I do not relish this case." I sensed that he sincerely meant that part about the relish. His obvious empathy made me feel better. Fortunately, I was blameless. I called him back saying, "Syd, I have some info proving your client has no case." He may not relish this news. Given that Syd did not relish suing me, indubitably Syd and I both relished the outcome.

Another positive trait we practise is civility. We generally refer to opposing counsel as "my friend" or sometimes the more elevated version, "my learned friend." We may oftentimes, given the circumstances, feel like deviating from this respectful address, but I have never witnessed a lawyer straying and launching a tirade of anatomical- or biological-based remarks towards an opponent (or a learned one).

I would like to see similar civility, say, in hockey: "Mr. Referee, this notable gentleman charged at me almost propelling me over the boards. I do object."

And our profession's self-policing mechanisms are stringent on steroids. The law society once audited me, and their main complaint was that I had money sitting around in my client trust account without activity for over two years. My bad. I thought it best not to ask the auditor whether I could use some of it to treat a few lawyers, thereby enabling us to eat and drink as friends.

Which gets me to honesty and integrity. Most of us are as straight as the proverbial arrow. Once during my early days of practice, I had a case with one Williams, who had a reputation of being a difficult bully. We both wanted to adjourn a court motion set for the next morning. However, one of the lawyers had to actually attend court and advise the judge of the late adjournment request. The courthouse was out of town, and it was a nasty winter week. I telephoned Williams and with the expected magnanimity, he demanded that I go. I suggested a coin toss. He hesitated and replied, "OK, but only if he flips the coin." He also graciously insisted on calling the toss. I agreed and got my galoshes ready. I heard him call "heads," followed by a couple of expletives. They rivalled anything those hockey players might utter. He made the court appearance. (I guess he did not relish losing the coin toss.) Though I saved the trip, to my greater delight Williams was an honest bully.

Our profession has much to be proud of. One commentary on our *Rules of Professional Conduct* notes, "A lawyer's conduct should reflect favourably on the legal profession; inspire the confidence, respect, and trust of clients and of the community; and avoid even the appearance of impropriety." In other words, we have not only to be good but always look good as well. The world counts on us. I'm sure we all welcome this mantle of honour.

In retrospect I'm glad I never told those undertakers I was spending my summers working my way through the "Collège de Québec des Mortuaires." All good. And when people think about lawyers, what likely quickly comes to mind is a courtroom and a trial. Let us now go to court and see what this is all about.

CHAPTER NINETEEN

See You in Court—Here We Are

"I was never ruined but twice; once when I lost a law-
suit and once when I won one."

~ Voltaire

What happens in the courtroom? Obviously, justice happens here. Criminal where people are tried for allegedly doing bad things, or civil where folks litigate against one another, usually for money. I will have more to say soon about the justice part.

The courtroom is composed of a number of characters, in addition to the lawyers of course, who make up the team, or rather the "perhaps" landscape since they do not all get paid for being there. And some of these characters are strange, including that mystery strange little old man I mentioned in the introduction. More about him later. Let's start with the judge. (The judge can be strange but this is not a requirement.)

THE JUDGE

The judge is almost always a lawyer, meaning he or she went to law school. As we have seen, this experience does not often mean much. More important, we just hope the judge has some common sense. What is crucial is that the judge be neutral and objective. Ask a judge, and the reply will be, "Of course I'm neutral and objective; I'm a judge.

OK. But is it possible that judges have personal idiosyncrasies that colour their objective lenses? For example, I once had a nonjury dog-bite trial. I opened with, "My client was delivering a pizza when suddenly the defendant's dog, a Rhodesian Ridgeback, lunged and bit him. Rhodesian Ridgebacks were actually bred in Africa to hunt lions. They're highly dangerous."

At that point, the judge interjected, "Ahem. No, they're not. My daughter has a Rhodesian Ridgeback, and he's as gentle as a lamb." I cannot say my confidence in the case did a 180-degree turn. However, I suddenly wished I had opted for a trial by jury. At least there would have been a chance that one or two jurors might have once worked for Domino's. We lost this case, His Honour finding no evidence of the dog's predisposition to maul unsuspecting deliverers of pizza. Judicial bias? Perish the thought.

Speaking of dogs, my colleague and mentor, Hank, had a case where a Shih Tzu bolted and ran up, growling, at his client's leg. The client "slightly" kicked the pooch, resulting in getting charged with some cruelty-against-animals offense.

Hank, to give his articling student, Alvin, some court experience, sent him to enter a guilty plea, expecting a small fine. Alvin returned to the office, tail between his legs (proverbially speaking). Gasping, he reported that the judge hammered the client with seven days in the slammer. Hank told the astonished Alvin that the judge was a former director of the SPCA. Can you fault the judge? At least the student got that court experience.

Often the judges' backgrounds are more known. We had a judge I'll call ID (no relation to the Freudian ID). Here, ID stands for "impaired driving." He was a curmudgeon well-known for his aversion to drunk drivers.

Although judges routinely issued a fine for a first-offense, ID would generally hit the inebriated driver with incarceration. No informed lawyer would enter a guilty plea before him. Shakespeare's iconic plea, "The quality of mercy is not strained," would have no meaning for him. Tweety had a better chance of getting a break from Sylvester.

We had another judge who was assaulted by thugs who also stole his prized Omega watch. Did this incident affect his objectivity? I doubt it of course. Maybe? I once witnessed a mugging sentencing in his court. The Crown Attorney read a facts synopsis. I don't know the outcome as I had to scoot off to another courtroom, but the last part I heard was the judge saying, "Rolex? That's even more valuable than an Omega." Whatever happened, I'll bet the defendants' lawyer learned a valuable lesson. Know your judge.

I had previously mentioned that elderly judge originating from England who had served as an admiral in the Royal Navy. Judge O, for Ocean, had a soft spot for sailors and things maritime. Wise lawyers would be sure to bring out any of their clients' maritime connections they could muster, however remote.

Unfortunately, aside from the client I mentioned earlier who originated from the Maritimes, whenever I appeared before O, none of my other clients had had any sailor experiences. On one occasion, my client James, who came from Saskatchewan, had never seen an ocean. I felt marooned. The best I could think of in addressing sentencing would have been, "George hails from Saskatchewan, but he always wished he had been born in Vancouver." I was tempted to import something seaworthy, but I never had the guts to open with, "Your Honour, ahoy!"

Which brings us to what do we do if we come across a judge where we sense some reasonable apprehension of inherent bias? First, we have those situations where you have no clue of any of the judge's inherent biases. Taking my dog-bite case, I was completely in the dark. It would have been great to be able to question the judge at the outset:

"Your Honor, before we begin, does your daughter own a Rhodesian Ridgeback?"

"Yes, counsel. How do you know?"

"Wild guess, sir. I request you recuse yourself."

No such luck. And even when you do know the judge's negative biases, you may have few options. I doubt it will help much if in the sentencing of a robber client you told that judge who got mugged, "At least he didn't take the victim's watch."

What to do? Mark Twain said, "A good lawyer knows the law; a clever one takes the judge to lunch." I don't quite recommend you try this in your courtroom. However, I actually ran across Judge O, the admiral, at a reception. I cautiously navigated the chat to his naval career, commenting, "I believe more young people today should join the navy." Judge O agreed proudly, adding as we clinked glasses of sherry, "It turns boys into men."

I was hoping that he would remember our short "cheers" meeting the next time I might appear before him with a case similar to the one with James. I visualized Judge O rolling his eyes when I mentioned that land-locked province, eyeballing the client, and asserting sternly, "Sir, I should send you to jail, but I am moved by your unfortunate surrounding residential circumstances and your fine lawyer's cogent comments. There will be a fine of $50." However, I never appeared before him again. Then again, would it have mattered? After all, judges are objective and neutral.

I have mentioned common sense, neutrality, and objectivity. Have I mentioned nastiness? I retired from my litigation practice in the Greater Toronto Area after over four decades of slugging it out as a sole practitioner in a busy litigation practice. I often wanted to express my thoughts about judges in general. All lawyers know they are supposed to act with courage and candour. Given that my court appearances were usually before a judge, I thought it wise to exercise restraint on that courage part and certainly more so on the candour part of it.

Now that I no longer experience these privileged appearances, I feel I can address these issues confidently and without fear of repercussions. What can we reasonably say about judges, according them due process? Offhand, most judges are a pleasure to deal with. They listen and they treat lawyers and clients with respect. But, firstly, they all generally start off as lawyers. However, the lawyers naively expect the judges to remember those stressful days of slugging it out in front of hard-nosed judges. The problem is that some judges develop a severe case of "hard noseitis" also known as "judgitis," which in short is Greek for "Move over Louis XIV, I'm on the bench now."

This is not totally surprising. They have the power to incarcerate felons, financially enrich or destroy litigants, and even overrule political leaders. And unlike the late comedian Rodney Dangerfield, they command respect. Bucketloads of it. Right off the bat, a judge's entry into the courtroom is preceded by a registrar bellowing, "Order! All rise." We lawyers and other mortals never get that type of greeting, not even when we enter a Walmart.

Then there are the obligatory judicial addresses. In England, and not long ago here, we used to address a High Court judge as, "My Lord." A female judge was "My Lady."

I once witnessed a police officer calling the justice "Your Honour," to which the judge responded, "We'll wait 'til you get it properly." Things actually went down from there as the officer nervously tried by saying, "Sorry, Your Worship." We waited. Fortunately, opposing counsel eventually whispered the magic phrase to the flustered policeman and the trial continued. And back in my McGill law-school days in Montreal, the salutation to a High Court justice was, "Monseigneur." When I hear that, I almost expect the judge's court entrance to be heralded by a platoon of flags and trumpets.

I actually had the experience of acting as a judge at our law school's moot court. I am reasonably humble, but I will say the position, even temporary, can go to your head. Those monseigneurs sounded rather melodic. I was tempted to ask counsel to repeat some of their submissions. But judgitis can go to the judges' heads, turning them nasty. I have seen judges who are sticklers for the garb the lawyers sport. One insisted that male lawyers appearing before him wear either black or gray pants. If some unsuspecting lawyer appeared in brown pants, Justice X would interrupt him saying, "I can't hear you." The poor lout would just crank up his voice a few decibels. Before long some colleague would whisper to him that not his voice was the pariah, but rather the colour of his pants. Justice X actually used to stand down the case. (I call him "X" as I still fear him and I don't want to have to engage the services of the witness protection program.)

Then there is the critic judge, who obliterates the client's confidence in his lawyer. I once witnessed a newbie lawyer cross-examining a police officer in a drunk-driving case. The officer never mentioned smelling alcohol, but sure enough, the lawyer asked the cop that question. The judge, known for his rudeness to lawyers, interrupted, saying, "Counsel, you are doing a great job of convicting your client." He may as well have said, "Honey, I just shrunk your lawyer."

Many other judges are polite, but overdemanding. I have experienced judges who, as they announce the lunch break, will say something like, "Mr. Strigberger, I would like some law on that hearsay issue. I suggest you go to the library and help me." This judge no doubt ascribes to the scientific theory that lawyers don't have to eat. At least he does not add insult to injury by adding, "Bon appétit." That judge with the problem with the brown pants might have.

A major predicament lawyers often encounter is appearing before judges who never read the written materials. We'd spend hours honing an affidavit or factum or other brief, and you could just tell from the judge's stare that his most salient experience with your documents was a paper cut.

In addition to the respect, members of the judiciary enjoy incredible perks, including generous vacation time and pensions. And unlike the lawyers, they don't have to look for business. I have yet to see a sign at a bus shelter reading, "Justice William (Bill) Langley. Award winning judge." Perhaps the greatest perk is the ability to slip up. A judge blows it and the appellate court can correct the error. Even then, the judge is accorded respect in the Notice of Appeal, reading something like: "1. The learned judge erred in admitting as psychiatric evidence the testimony of Dr. Marvin Berman, who is actually a dermatologist." Slip up in the business world, and management gives you a pink slip. I doubt its contents contain the word "learned."

As I said, most judges do get it right (generally). But if there are any judges coming across this oration, and some of the lamentations apply to you, please do read it diligently. And be careful not to get a paper cut. And as the lawyers would say to suck up to the judge, all of which is submitted, respectfully of course.

Of interest is that judges have also dumped on fellow judges. The Ontario Court of Appeal in a case accused many judges of being too verbose, in effect accusing them of sounding like lawyers. The Ontario Court of Appeal noted that the reasons for the decision of many judges often amount to "factual data dumps." The court said that the documents it must deal with often contain a "blizzard of words." In this instance, I shall come to the assistance of the trial judges and say that this criticism is harsh and unwarranted. I sympathize with the trial judges. In my view it is a major challenge for a judge to find a good balance between dumping a verbal tsunami or being too skimpy. To quote Einstein, "Everything should be made as simple as possible but not simpler."

Let us examine the tasks each of the two levels of court have. Compared to the job of a trial judge, being an appeal court judge is a breeze. Firstly, let's remember that as all judges are also lawyers firstly, we are obsessive about getting it right and therefore cautious about oversimplification. Why then, for example, would lawyers draft a will as "Last Will and Testament. I give, devise, and bequeath." They can simply say: "My Will. My son Jeremy gets everything." Maybe for emphasis, they can add a "badda bing, badda boom." After all, all Jeremy wants to hear is, "What am I getting?" I'll bet he never even heard of the word bequeath. Beings lawyers therefore, the Court of Appeal should be the first to understand that verbosity is in our DNA.

And they should appreciate the challenges of the trial judge, who generally sits for days or weeks listening to all the evidence. He or she has to take copious notes and then cull it in order to write a fair and accurate decision to possibly make life easy for a potential appeals court justice. I don't know what the trial judge in that case did wrong. I'm sure he tried hard to keep it balanced. I doubt his factual data dump included information such as, "10:03 a.m. I took a sip of water. Ahhh. Good."

The appellate judges on the other hand do not review the appeal documents until a day or so before the hearing. Also, there are three judges. One or all can do the work and ask questions of the lawyers. Their choice. If a judge chooses to daydream and think about when the Toronto Blue Jays will win the World Series again, no problem. Just maybe doodle a bit to make it look as though he or she is absorbing the desperate lawyer's pitch.

After the argument of generally a half day or less, they can retire and one of them later gives reasons for their decision. The enviable part is that the other two judges can simply endorse the record with the words, "I agree." How balanced is that? I have never known a losing lawyer to ask one of these judges the obvious question, "Why?" I was tempted a few times to ask it, and to add, "What law school did you go to?" I'd call "I agree" a bird-size data dump. I suppose if time is tight, they can even just say, "Agree." It reminds me of that Woody Allen quote where he says something like, "I took a speed-reading course and read *War and Peace* in twenty minutes. It involves Russia."

Furthermore, the Court of Appeal panel judges can often quickly make up their minds on the merits of the appeal after the appellant lawyer's argument, and end it all, saying to the Respondent's lawyer, "We don't have to hear from you, Ms. Bailey."

How's that for simplicity? A trial judge can't get off that easy. I practised for over forty years and I always thought my clients were right. However, never did I have the pleasure of a trial judge agreeing with me without my having to say a word. (I will add, very often I thought my opponent's presentation of the evidence was a data dump.) There is definitely an inherent discomfort, to put it kindly, between these two levels of court. If we could access the minds of these judges, we would see what each level of the court really thinks about the other. I can only imagine what we would see. Let's have a look:

Waldo J. (trial judge)

This is an action by Jake Langley against Chez Vincent's Café for damages. The event took place on a fine summer day, July 13 last year, when the plaintiff decided to take his girlfriend, Celeste Barker, for lunch. The evidence is not in dispute that upon arrival the waiter, one Erik, asked the couple whether they wanted to eat indoors or outside on the terrace. Both Jake and Celeste agreed the weather was just too good to sit inside and they opted for the terrace.

They both proceeded to order a bowl of butternut squash soup. As Celeste was about halfway through her soup, Jake noticed something darkish floating around in the middle of his girlfriend's soup. He asked, "Honey, is that a fly in your soup?"

Celeste took a closer look, lifting the black object out of the soup with her spoon. After examining the suspect entity, and giving it a slight poke, she said, "Yes dear, it is." Upon hearing this news, Jake let out an ear-piecing shriek and ran off to the washroom, where he says he suffered a panic attack. He started to sweat profusely and pant quickly. He also started swearing in Russian, although he claims he does not even speak a word of Russian. Jake then apparently tried to commit suicide but his efforts were thwarted by the quick actions of the waiter, Erik, who managed to quickly pull Jake's leg out of the toilet bowl while the toilet was flushing.

This event, he says, proved to be too much for him. Shortly thereafter Jake started getting psychotherapy, which he still gets twice a week. The shock of seeing that fly was apparently so pervasive that not only did he vow never to eat soup again, but he also forthwith broke off his relationship with Celeste as he associated her with the fly in the soup. He then commenced this action for damages, including punitive and for nervous shock.

Let us deal first with liability. I must ask, was there a duty of care owed by Chez Vincent to the plaintiff? I have no doubt that there was. When a restaurant serves, it has a duty to ensure that it serves same sans flies. This case is on all fours with *Kingsley v. Soup for You*, although in that case the soup was cream of broccoli.

Next, the court must ask, was this duty breached? Once again, the answer must be yes. As Lord Mundane said in the Kingsley case, "Her Majesty's subjects have every reason to enjoy a fine potage without the intrusion of crawlers and creepers. And should one of these insects find their way into the soup, the court will find a breach of duty. And I so find a breach in this case."

I must then ask, did the breach of duty cause damage to the plaintiff? The evidence presented was that the plaintiff was a model of sound health prior to this incident. He was in fact an airline pilot, having flown commercial aircraft for Air Hotspots for over twenty years. Since the accident, he has been unable to resume flying. He claims that flying reminds him of the fly and that he cannot get into a cockpit anymore. There is clear causation.

Finally, the question is, was this damage remote? Evidence for the plaintiff was given by Professor Dieter von Himmel, of the University of Stuttgart, a renowned authority on the psychiatric effects upon victims of flies in their soup. Professor von Himmel testified that it is not unusual for these victims to transfer the event into other areas of their lives and to go into avoidance of anything that reminds them of the traumatic incident. The professor testified that this was well known to the British during World War II. In fact, Sir Winston Churchill personally ordered secret agents to go to cafés in Germany and drop flies into the soups of pilots serving in the Luftwaffe. It is a little-known secret that some seven hundred pilots who found these flies were so traumatized that they could no longer come within fifty metres of a Messerschmitt.

During cross-examination, Professor von Himmel also confirmed that indeed after seeing those flies in their soup, many of the German pilots started swearing in Russian. This behaviour in fact is known as the "St. Petersburg Syndrome," so named after the seventh assassination attempt on Rasputin, where his conspirators laced his lemonade with a litre of strychnine. In that case, Rasputin actually started swearing in Danish.

I find that the damage was not remote. To the contrary, it was clearly reasonably foreseeable. I accept the evidence of the plaintiff as to both liability and damages. In addition to special out-of-pocket damages, I assess general damages for pain and suffering at $150,000.

The plaintiff also claimed punitive damages. The plaintiff called the expert, Dr. Michael LaBarge, Chairman of Soupology at the University of the Western Maritimes. Dr. LaBarge testified that butternut squash has a well-known tendency to attract flies. I have no doubt that this information was known to the defendant restaurant. In fact, it tried hard to cover up this knowledge. Erik, under vigorous cross-examination, admitted the following damning facts:

Plaintiff's Counsel:

Sir, Vincent St. Pierre, the owner, testified that he did not know that butternut squash soup attracted flies. Is that statement correct?

Erik:

Not exactly sir. A week before he told the waiting staff to keep pushing the butternut even though it attracted flies as it yielded a larger profit margin than chicken soup.

I have no doubt the defendant sought to subdue this truth. The court must send out a clear message that this type of callous and egregious conduct will not be tolerated. I assess punitive damages in the amount of $500,000.

The defendant appealed. The Court of Appeal allowed the appeal with legal costs to the defendant at both court levels. There were no formal reasons given, but a document was found in the waste basket of Appellate Justice Elevated J.A. This document was discovered by the Registrar who entered His Honour's chambers after he heard the three justices hearing the appeal roar with laughter an entire afternoon. The document reads as follows:

Elevated J.A.:
This is an appeal of the decision of Waldo J.

A. Overview
This is another fly in the soup case. Buzz buzz.

B. Issue
Are the plaintiff's "damages" remote? And how.

C. Facts
This court did not have the benefit the learned trial judge had of seeing the witness and judging their demeanour. This small impediment however should not prevent us from usurping his functions. In fact, we find trial judges spend simply too much time listening to evidence for days on end. This actually taints their judgment as they may be swayed by what witnesses say. In the Court of Appeal, we can spend a few moments glossing over a factum or two and readily override the trial judge's decision. Once we get elevated to the Court of Appeal, we have the divine right to do so. There would hardly be a need for a Court of Appeal if we would not allow appeals. After all, three heads are better than one. And since we are a higher court, we can see the case from a better perspective than the trial judge can ever hope to do.

I. Analysis
The appellant argues that the choice was the customer's on whether or not to dine indoors or outdoors. It is a known fact that in the summertime, insects are apt to be crawling or flying about near where food is served in

the hope of finding a quick snack, or at least in the hope of ruining someone's picnic. In the case at bar, the learned trial judge, who should have been more learned, failed to pay any deference to the defendant's pleas of *volenti* or willingly taking the risk should the trial judge not understand this fundamental Latin principle. By choosing to sit outside in July, the plaintiff may as well have placed a large sign on his table reading, "Attention flies: butternut-squash soup this way."

Nor are we bound by the *Kingsley* case. It is a known fact that Lord Mundane did not even like soup. To His Lordship, fine dining was a pepperoni pizza. We are surprised that the learned trial judge did not take this into account in formulating his reasons.

Furthermore, as learned as the learned trial judge was, he completely ignored the legal effect of the waiver of liability. We refer to the sign next to the reception which reads, "Chez Vincent is not responsible for anything, however caused." The learned (ha ha) trial judge would have known this had he been more familiar with chapter 7 of *Williams on Waivers*, 14th edition. On page 143 the author notes, "It is trite law going back to the days of Edward I that an innkeeper need only warn his customers of the potential for harm. This constitutes an absolute waiver of liability. Nor can the customer say he was illiterate and could not read the sign." We would therefore allow the appeal as the plaintiff's case fails on liability.

And although we need not decide on the issue of damages, we feel that if we do make some comments, it would agitate the trial judge more. So let's do it.

The Court of Appeal should not interfere lightly with the decisions of quantum of the trial judge, unless they are totally out of line. This court finds that an award of $150,000 is not only totally out of line but totally out to lunch. (Let nobody say that the justices of this court do not have a sense of humour.) How can a little fly in someone else's soup cause so much emotional trauma? A restaurant patron is supposed to have reasonable fortitude to withstand the reasonable vicissitudes of life.

With all due respect to Professor von Himmel, whose reputation is well known to this court, we view this as a case about trifles, i.e., *de minimis*. We do not know what the most learned trial judge was thinking about, but perhaps before rendering his decision he must have consumed a bowl of soup consisting of strange mushrooms. Just where was Waldo?

Furthermore, it is a well-known fact that Rasputin, after consuming that lemonade with strychnine, started speaking not Danish but Yiddish. Among other things, he accused his would-be assassins of having *chutzpah*.

Nor would we allow punitive damages. Punitive damages entail that element of malice or deliberate conduct on the part of the defendant. We do not see any malice or deliberate conduct. Nor could the trial judge reasonably have drawn that conclusion merely from the fact that one of the plaintiff's witnesses saw Erik collecting live flies in a jar and talking to them. Most importantly, this court does not like it if a simple trial judge awards punitive damages. We like our court to set the law on this subject.

II. Disposition

We allow the appeal with legal costs to the appellant throughout.

It seems that the undisclosed reasons came to the attention of the learned trial judge Waldo J. He then made some notes in his diary about the Court of Appeal decision:

October 13

I have just read the draft reasons of that place that calls itself the highest court in the province. It is so high in fact that I fear that there must be a shortage of oxygen at that level, which may account for some of the decisions rendered by its justices. As trial judges do not get a chance to rebut or otherwise comment when that court overrules one of us, I must simply content myself with penning my thoughts in my diary, in the hope that somebody finds my diary.

"I note that this trial ran over two weeks. I listened to evidence given by both sides. I noticed the demeanor in which the witnesses testified and

I made my findings on credibility. I actually saw the litigants/clients. For the benefit of the Court of Appeal, *Brown's Law Dictionary* defines a client as 'the person who gets hurt and hires a lawyer to pursue an action, or the person who causes the damage and hires a lawyer to defend the claim. The former is called the plaintiff and the latter the defendant.'"

These are usually live people who walk and talk. The Court of Appeal generally does not know what they look like. But they do exist.

That Court upstairs usually works in a pack of three, although one of its members generally does the talking and the other two take a time out. So, whereas the trial judge often listens to the evidence for days on end, a Court of Appeal judge can usually dispose of the case in half an hour. I am really not sure just what the other two justices on the panel do, but for Christmas I intend to send a few of them Sudoku puzzles and knitting materials.

In the "Langley" case, the Court did not accept my findings of liability or damages. Trial judges are often asked whether they are resentful when this higher court tosses out their rulings. I say this. We are professionals. We are neutral. Why would we be resentful? Judges do not know the meaning of that word. If a higher court overrules us, we accept it in stride. After all, that court's justices do get an unobstructed view of the case as they see it from their ivory tower. And they no doubt further aim to sharpen their skills by taking continuing-education courses. I understand that in fact next week the justices are attending a course entitled, "Twenty-five new ways of saying "I concur." This is huge.

I have to go now. I am about to start a trial. I will not bother explaining to the Court of Appeal the meaning of that word. Aren't we glad that judges are human?

The Court of Appeal should appreciate the diligent efforts of trial judges to keep it balanced and simple. Then again, in both courts judges are only judges, not Einsteins. Badda bing, badda boom.

But what do non-lawyers think about judges? Is ignorance often bliss for lay people having contact with the legal system? I have noticed that non-lawyers enjoy a much more relaxed attitude with the judicial environment than we lawyers do. Lay people have qualms expressing themselves with complete candor. For example, when a judge enters the courtroom, he or she takes a short bow towards the body of the court and the lawyers return the compliment, taking a bow back.

I noticed a number of times lay people look at one another, emitting a smile. One client gave the judge a thumbs up. The judge looked puzzled, as if she thought, "I must have done something right already." Many lawyers also tend to immediately throw dubious flattering phrases at the judge. They announce their names saying something like, "If it please Your Honour, my name is Lawrence Coopersmith representing the plaintiff." This salutation reminds me of that song those Siamese cats sing in Disney's *Lady and the Tramp*, "We are Siamese if you please. We are Siamese if you don't, please."

Clients will often resort to comments evoked by emotion. I once represented a gentleman in an impaired driving charge. He was a proud WWII navy veteran who obviously had experienced more trying situations than this indictment. In the midst of a robust cross-examination by the prosecutor, he said with utter confidence, "You are harassing me with all these questions. I spent years in a submarine, dodging depth charges; there is nothing you can do to me." The young prosecutor was a bit taken aback, obviously shaken. The judge, who seemed somewhat bored up to this point, suddenly perked up. He said to the client, "Mr. Cerniek, we do acknowledge your service to our country, but please just answer Ms. Fitzmichael's questions and we shall all be out of here soon."

I thought to myself that a lawyer could never go off on a tangent like that. It would, however, indeed be refreshing and liberating to be able to say to a judge, "Your Honour, you say my witness's comment is hearsay, but you must admit this testimony, as after all, he served for three years as a navy commando." I somehow doubt whether the judge would then say, "Actually, counsel serving as a commando is an exception to the hearsay rule."

I also recall a matrimonial case where the judge ordered my client, a musician, to pay his wife some arrears of support. My client, Rick, did not like this ruling and he told the judge outright, "For that amount of money I can get myself a new set of drums."

The judge added that in default of payment, Rick would have to spend some time in jail. I cringed as Rick was behind in paying my fees. Though tempted to express myself with the client's candor, I restrained myself from saying, "Your Honour, with that amount of money Rick can pay off my outstanding fees account." Where is the justice?

Lay people have no problems telling the judge outright what they think of the judicial system. I was in court once when the case before mine involved a short hearing where the judge had to assess a legal bill between a lawyer and her client. The client wasted no time jumping on the judge saying, "I know the outcome exactly. You judges and lawyers stick together like glue." The judge actually went on the defensive, presumably trying to refute the client's suspicions about any possible systematic bias. I don't know if he succeeded. I did, however, think to myself that I would have liked to be before this judge in that case where Rick still owed me that money.

Lay people's relaxed attitude towards judges is also apparent out of the courtroom. One of our Toronto courthouses houses trial courtrooms on the upper floors of a high-rise. There are no separate elevators for the judges. During a break as my client and I were about to enter an elevator, we noticed the trial judge heading for the same elevator. I hit my brakes as did other colleagues, allowing the judge to enter by herself. My client was surprised. He said to me, "That was our judge. Why didn't we ride down with her? We could have explained that traffic signal to her better." This comment had a couple of colleagues who overheard it giggling. The truth probably is that we all likely shared this unattainable fantasy. After all we're lawyers.

And what happens when we come across judges out of the court-house? As lawyers, do we unwittingly deify judges? Judges often have lunch at restaurants near the courthouse. I do not recall ever coming near one and engaging him or her in a dialogue. I thought of that Old Testament scene with Lot's wife. I almost felt that if I did, I would instantly turn into a pillar of salt.

A client of mine once noticed my discomfort. When I told him there was a judge sitting at a nearby table, he said, "Wow! I'll bet you thought judges don't have to eat." Judges certainly can wield power, deciding whether you get money or freedom. Lawyers are more uptight about this than the public. I think of that comment by that iconic comedienne and former film star Mae West in a courtroom scene in *My Little Chickadee* where the judge says: "Are you trying to show contempt for this court?" Mae West in her character as Flower Belle responds, "On the contrary your Honor, I'm doing my best to hide it." Now what are the chances of a lawyer ever coming up with a gem response like that? Are we lawyers too invested in the system? Amen. And speaking of Einsteins, let me say something about juries. Grrr ...

THE JURY

The Jury Is Out—Big Time

Juries first scared me at the age nine. How? I grew up in Montreal, the son of immigrants from Belgium. One day my late father, a humble tailor, received a letter with an impressive-looking logo of the scales of justice. My dad, whose literary skills did not approximate his ability to alter a fine pair of trousers, asked me to read and translate it. I noticed the word "jury," whatever that meant. I suspected it had nothing to do with hockey.

Our neighbour, a grade-school teacher read the letter and told my dad he was being summoned to court for jury duty. My father trembled, asking why he was being summoned to court as he had done nothing wrong. After offering my father a drink, the neighbour explained what a jury was all about, noting that he would be a vital component of the justice system.

After a second drink, my father settled down. However, after further deliberation, he asked the neighbour to write a letter requesting an exemption on the grounds that he could not read or speak English. (Back in those days in Quebec this shortcoming was still considered a deficiency.) The exemption was readily granted.

Interestingly, my father considered this event a positive experience. He even kept the summons, viewing it as a certificate of honour. If anybody ever questioned his integrity, he would proudly say, "Hey, I was even called for a jury." We once experienced a burglary and when the insurance adjuster arrived to investigate, as the discussion heated up, my father asked me to fetch the letter.

My first observation of a jury, however, was watching *Perry Mason* every week. He and prosecutor Hamilton Burger would duke it out in front of twelve people, and generally he didn't even need a jury to secure an acquittal. The real murderer usually was close by, either on the witness stand or in the body of the courtroom. Perry Mason brilliantly figured that out, getting the culprit to cry out a confession to the murder. That certainly saved the jury some work. I often visualized my father sitting in that jury box, thinking that his English language proficiency there likely would not have made a difference (like in Quebec today).

My real jury experience happened only after my Bar call, and I found the system daunting. We all had a good idea of the local judges' dispositions, from a hanging judge to a lenient judge who understood the accused was not a villain. When he jumped into a crowd swinging that machete, he "acted out of character," merely straying. But how do you deal with twelve individuals you know little about other than their occupations? For starters, I was uneasy about juror selection in that the names are drawn out of a drum, like bingo: "G-57, Melvin Lubovsky, plumber."

Although I had my share of jury trials, I preferred trials by judge alone. And yes, I know going back to the *Magna Carta* it is called a "jury of your peers." These days, we refer to these peers as "twelve folks standing in line with you at a Tim Hortons." I generally have little in common with most of these guys unless they order a medium black coffee and a maple donut. I just never felt comfortable with laypeople making possible life-altering judgments. When I'm on an airplane (pre- and post-COVID-19), I prefer leaving all judgments to the pilot. I'd get nervous seeing a panel of Tim Horton aficionados in the cockpit during a storm saying to the captain, "Take it down 2,000 feet."

And yes, I did watch *12 Angry Men*, where one juror slowly convinces the other eleven to alter their initial votes of guilty. This is encouraging, but what are your chances of lucking out and drawing Henry Fonda as a juror?

Another concern is the way the evidence is often vetted before a jury. First, there is the *voir dire*. Precious time is spent arguing admissibility while the jury is banished like a child about to get exposed to an R-rated movie. Giving the jury some credit, it does not take Sherlock Holmes to figure out that the arresting cop may have also searched further and found in the defendant's trunk, in addition to the machete, something like a .44 Magnum. A reasonable suspicion.

More concerning, in American courts where if some improper testimony is blurted out, the judge will admonish the jury saying, "The jury will disregard that evidence. I order that it be stricken from the record." I am sure that fixes it. I can see the jury deliberating and the foreman saying, "Now, does the defendant have a propensity for violence? Remember, we really did not hear anything about that .44 Magnum." We just never find out what goes on in that jury room. Our judges tell the jury the lawyers will talk to them at the beginning and the end of the trial, and that's it. Other than that, no chatting, not even a greeting.

I actually was at a mall food court once and saw a former juror walking towards me. I recalled the jury hammering me in that trial. She spotted me and immediately made a large side sprint avoiding my gaze. That was social distancing pre-COVID-19. I noticed she went over to the Tim Hortons. She did not order a black coffee and a maple donut. Had I had this vital knowledge before jury selection, I would have challenged her acceptance for cause. Successfully no doubt. Obviously, she was not a peer of mine.

I never overcame my discomfort with juries. At least my dad appreciated them. And here's a shocker. Did you know lawyers and even judges in the United States are eligible for jury duty?

Judge, Jury, Me, and Me

Lawyers and judges serving as jurors? Unthinkable in Canada. It recently came to my attention that in the U.S. not only lawyers but even judges are fair game for jury duty. I started ruminating, and my mind drifted into the following fantasy. What if a judge's number were to come up to serve jury duty for his or her own court? And what if he diligently wore two different hats, like the multi-role character Poo-Bah from Gilbert and Sullivan's *The Mikado*? I extended this fantasy further, visualizing what just might go through the mind of this person compartmentalizing totally as each of judge and juror in, say, a criminal arson trial. What would their respective diary entries look like?

Monday

Judge: Jury selection is done. The lawyers did a thorough job in vetting the prospective jurors. I pity these jurors. They have to show up here and during these blizzard conditions for a paltry $50 or so per day. The justice system isn't perfect. But at least I earn a handsome six-figure annual salary.

Juror: Both the defence lawyer and the district attorney were content with my being on the jury; however, they each grilled me beforehand, asking me whether I ever made a fire-related insurance claim. How's that relevant? I now have to spend days travelling here during this winter blast, earning a measly $50 per day. That's probably less per hour than a Walmart greeter. Jury duty, bah!

Tuesday

Judge: The lawyers each presented their opening statements. They were concise. The prosecution then called witnesses, including the defendant's accountant who testified that the defendant's business had been in the red and he was refused additional bank loans. I noticed the defendant was a bit shifty in his seat and judging by his nervous demeanor I would say he did torch his warehouse to access insurance monies.

Juror: Do these attorneys get paid by the word? They rambled on for what seemed like hours. The prosecution called evidence alleging the defendant needed more money. What does that prove? I'll say the same thing given that the government only pays me that $50 dollars per diem. I carefully observed the defendant and although he seemed a bit edgy, he clearly emitted an aura of innocence.

Wednesday

Judge: There were a number of objections by both lawyers to much of the testimony. A couple of times I had to send the jury out of the courtroom to hear, in their absence, the argument on these objections, including the one by defence counsel when a prosecution witness insurance adjuster blurted out that he visited the defendant after the fire and noticed three jerricans in his garage. I disallowed this testimony and asked the jurors to disregard this comment as it was being stricken from the record. I trust the jurors found something productive to do while waiting in the jury room.

Juror: These lawyers certainly made a raucous scene today, jumping over one another with objections. The judge really flipped when that insurance guy mentioned those jerricans, after which he kicked us out of the courtroom. He later said this testimony was stricken from the record and admonished us to forget hearing anything about those jerricans. Right!

Already forgotten. Ha ha! At least we spent our time out in the jury room productively—playing Wordle.

Thursday

Judge: All the evidence is in. Both lawyers made their closing arguments to the jury. Once again, they were concise and to the point as they tried to persuade the jurors of their positions. I then gave my charge to the jury, telling them in order to find the defendant guilty they must find guilt beyond a reasonable doubt. I noted that they are the masters of the facts, namely, which facts they should accept or reject.

The jury, then sequestered, will have to spend their time in the jury room until they reach a unanimous verdict. I do expect the jurors to come up with a quick conviction as, to me, the guy came across as guilty as sin. However, I did tell the jurors that if the hours extend without a verdict, accommodations would be made for lodging at a hotel. At least I get to sleep in the comfort of my own home.

Juror: These lawyers have little regard for our convenience and intelligence. They just rambled on and on. Don't they know what the seat can't endure, the mind can't absorb? The judge then ranted on with his charge saying it was up to the jury to decide what facts to accept. Any idiot knows that.

We were then sent off to the jury room, but given the hour, we were transferred to a hotel for the night. Not fun. Jury duty certainly is not rewarding economically. I asked the hotel staff but they told me that since I was not paying for the room, I was not eligible to receive the hotel's reward points. Ugh!

Friday

Judge: I expected a quick jury guilty verdict, but I was totally surprised that the jury returned to the courtroom speedily but with a verdict of not guilty. Didn't they listen to the evidence? What do they do in the jury room, play Wordle?

Juror: My initial hunch about the defendant's innocence of arson was right. We all found him not guilty. As instructed by the judge we did not take into account that evidence stricken from the record about those jerricans. Anyhow, the defendant likely used the gasoline to fill up his snowblower. What a vision!

Fortunately, here in Canada lawyers are in no way eligible for jury duty. However, the fact that the system in the U.S. allows even judges to so serve has piqued my interest and I would readily visit a courtroom with a judge on the jury, even if the trial were running during the course of a vigorous blizzard. OK, juries, bah!

D. That Strange Mystery Man

Now for that strange mystery man. As promised. This character is usually an elderly gentleman who sits to the right of the judge a step down on the bench. You usually see him (or used to when I practised) in the Superior Court. He looks distinguished, a dead ringer for Jeeves the butler. He does not say anything nor for that matter do anything except occupy that nook in the bench. I suppose he is an important part in the justice system. How important? I think of poet John Milton, who said, "They also serve who only stand and wait." This gentleman only sits and waits. I would say, to me his status is at least one rung above most politicians. Bravo. But what about a most important player in the legal system. Essential character; the witness.

E. Send In the Witnesses

It was a cold Canadian winter morning. But let me get back to that in a moment. The success of your case often gets down to three things: witnesses, witnesses, and witnesses. The concept of witnesses goes back over 3,000 years, where "Thou shalt not bear false witness" makes its debut in the Ten Commandments. Witnesses must have been important then. Where would our profession be without them now?

Now back to that cold Canadian winter morning. I was about to enter a restaurant to enjoy a fine Sunday brunch when suddenly I slipped and fell on a large patch of ice right at the entrance. As I lay there in agony, a gentleman helped me up, saying, "Careful, the walkway is a skating rink." That sage comment was an understatement. I would say that actually this was the closest I ever came to being an involuntary participant in the Ice Follies.

He alerted the restaurant, and a lady came out and dumped a bucket of salt on the *de facto* outdoor arena (sort of Latin I guess, meaning actual but not intended to be). I asked for the man's contact information. He handed me his business card, noting that he was a financial advisor. This is the first time I actually accepted a business card from yet another financial advisor. And it was a good thing I did. The insurance company eventually interviewed him and as the adjuster put it to me, "There is some corroboration here. We should be able to settle this case."

But not all of us are lawyers, appreciating the importance of witnesses. I had a client once who tripped over a protruding piece of lumber at a national chain hardware store. Apparently two customers who witnessed the event offered their contacts to the client but the manager who came by said it wasn't necessary and told them to leave. I wonder whether the store presents a course for staff on risk management and when they get to unfavourable witnesses, the manual reads, "Shoo them away."

Being a witness can be stressful, even for lawyers. A client once sued a prominent litigation lawyer on a home-renovation contract. The lawyer made the mistake of representing himself. In the middle of my client's testimony, the lawyer jumped up and shouted, "That's not true." The judge turned to him and said, "Now, now, Mr. Sullivan, you know the drill. You'll get your opportunity to try to get to the truth."

Then again, some witnesses not being familiar with the process are not stressed at all. They do not even realize who is who in the courtroom. An elderly client of mine at a trial once testified in a very low voice. The judge had trouble hearing him, especially as he was facing the opposing lawyer during cross-examination. The judge interrupted, saying, "Mr. Moscovitch, can you please look at me and speak a bit louder. I can't hear you." The witness replied, "It's OK. I'm not talking to you. I'm only talking to him." Moscovitch wasn't stressed (unlike Sullivan). Fortunately, the judge heard enough to grant us judgment.

Expert witnesses can be intimidating. One of my first trials involved a small two-seater hovercraft that mysteriously sank in a lake at a summer camp on its maiden voyage. My client and a teen camper were aboard. Fortunately, they were not hurt. After retrieving it from the lake, they noticed a small fist size hole in the hovercraft's hull. The client claimed that some rocks at the bottom of the lake must have caused the hole. Without photographing the damage, he hastily hitched it up and returned it to the vendor. The vendor photographed the hull noting a large gaping aperture somewhat resembling the Arc de Triomphe. He insisted my client crashed the hovercraft into some rocks. Surprise?

At trial, the vendor presented an impressive expert witness involved in designing the hovercraft. This expert was both a marine architect and an aeronautical engineer. We were talking a one-man NASA. He was a daunting, distinguished looking gentleman, resembling Sir Anthony Hopkins. I knew I was in trouble as he was sporting a navy-blue blazer bearing a crest of a colourful hot air balloon hovering over a mini-submarine.

I was mortified. Back then there was no obligation for a party to give the opposition a witness "will say." Trials were the Wild West. Trial by ambush was OK. The fly-and-float guru testified using scientific references, such as the Archimedes principle on buoyancy. He was adamant that absent trauma, this hovercraft was unsinkable.

My cross-examination was brief as the only science I remembered was some high-school physics, such as that the specific gravity and density of water was one. I did not think it would help my case much to ask whether Archimedes ever experimented with a hovercraft. I recall thinking that David had a better shot of beating Goliath. At least he was armed with a slingshot.

The judge surprisingly returned a verdict for the plaintiff. He was especially impressed by the testimony of that teen camper witness who said when looking at the vendor's photograph, opening his hands widely, "There was a hole there, but it wasn't *that* big!"

I learned a useful lesson regarding litigation, namely, not to be afraid of any witness, including some hot-shot expert sporting a navy-blue blazer bearing a crest with the likes of a mini-submarine hovering over a hot air balloon. Which gets us to the expert witness.

These are the witnesses who are allowed to express opinions on the facts. There are experts on everything from medical to economic, to guys with navy-blue blazers bearing the crest of a hot-air balloon and submarine. They are supposed to be objective and professional. But are they actually hired guns? The legal system's hit men?

In most jurisdictions they are supposed to prepare a report setting out their findings and expert opinions. They are expected to be objective. In Ontario for example, experts must, under the Rules of Practice and Procedure, deliver a certificate attesting to their impartiality. Then again, I suppose that some naïve people expect Foghorn Leghorn to peacefully coexist in the same yard with that dog. Not surprisingly in any one case, their respective opinions are on the opposite ends of the spectrum. I have noted, for example, that most psychiatric reports will assess the same accident victim diametrically opposed. For example, let's therefore take a case of a fiftyish year-old European woman who was a restaurant worker, but who had not been able to resume work since her car accident. The psychiatric reports to the respective lawyers might read as follows:

Dueling Experts
The plaintiff's medical assessment

I am an Associate Professor of psychiatry at the University of Toronto, with a special interest in chronic pain.

Visit: Your client Ludmilla arrived fifteen minutes early. This suggests someone who is very responsible. She was dressed casually, wearing blue jeans, obviously not being pretentious.

The catastrophic accident: Ludmilla was a vivid historian. She described that she was stopped when suddenly she was struck forcefully from the rear by a cement truck. She related, "I thinking I hit by atomic bomb. I dead for sure."

Personal history: She advises that she was born and raised in Hungary, the youngest of eight children. Her mother was a seamstress there. She was a heavy smoker. Her father, was a shepherd from rural Greece who went to seek his fortune in Budapest. He also dabbled in bicycle repairs. He was an altruistic gentleman, spending all his spare time asking people if he could fix their flat bicycle tires. Ludmilla is presently married to Victor, the owner of Victor's €Deli, in Toronto. Until the accident she assisted her husband in running the deli.

Examination: She had good eye contact. She is constantly in pain. She has had to stop working at the deli as, "I no longer able to lift anything. Even a pastrami sandwich with a pickle—no way—I feel useless." When asked to count backwards by sevens from 100, she got stuck at 90. I handed her a facial tissue as her eyes started to moisten.

Impressions: There is no doubt that this pleasant lady suffers from depression and severe chronic pain syndrome. Like her father, she was a workaholic who demanded 100%, or rather 107%, from herself. Now she is totally disabled from working. Her condition is entirely attributable to the serious motor-vehicle accident. The prognosis is guarded.

I trust you will find this objective report in order.

Sincerely,

C. Jackson Smithfield, M.D.

F. The Defence Medical Assessment

I am an associate professor of psychiatry at the University of Toronto, with a special interest in malingering. I read the medical brief that you sent along, including the report of Dr. Smithfield. I shall say no more about his report. I'll confine mine to non-fiction.

Visit: The subject woman arrived fifteen minutes early. This demonstrates pre-existing chronic anxiety. She just can't wait to get her hands on that insurance money. The subject was dressed sloppily in blue jeans, trying to impress me of her humility.

The Incident (???): She says that she was fully stopped when she was allegedly tapped by another vehicle. I can't imagine someone this anxious actually stopping for anything. She exaggerated, magnifying the size of the offending vehicle, adamant that it was a cement truck. When I asked her once again what type of car it was, she insisted it was a cement truck. She was non-repentant. She then said in describing the light jolt, "I dead for sure." She said this with the air of certainty that only a malingerer uses.

Personal History: It's obvious the subject learned her greed from her parents. Her father gave up the tranquil life of being a shepherd in Greece to carry on with cross-border contraband of stolen bicycle parts. It was the least he could do to keep his neurotic wife in her lavish smoking habit. The subject was the youngest of eight children, a spoiled brat no doubt.

Examination: Her eye contact was non-existent as she kept on burying her face in a Kleenex tissue. She was very hostile and anxious when I grabbed away the box of Kleenex and hid it in my microwave oven. She indicated she could do nothing at all at her husband's deli. "I completely useless." However, not surprisingly, on further questioning she was readily able to count pastrami sandwiches by sevens, from 100 down to 91. And to avoid any misunderstanding, I asked her three times whether indeed her father knew how to fix bicycles and she was adamant that he did.

Impressions: This lady is your classic malingerer. She falls squarely within the parameters of the F.T. (Fakers' Test). I speak of course of the seminal test developed by noted psychiatrist Professor August Strondenberg of the University of Gothenburg. We have a perfect match with all of the Professor's DSM-XVL indicia, which lead to the inescapable conclusion of malingering:

1. Her father was a disenchanted shepherd who developed a fetish with bicycles,

2. Her mother was chain smoking seamstress,

3. The subject spent years working in a delicatessen,

4. aid subject's favourite number is 7, and

5. She married a man called Victor who as the name suggests is a megalomaniac.

I have no doubt that once this lawsuit ends, the subject will achieve a complete recovery of these alleged injuries.

I trust you will find this unbiased report in order.

Sincerely,
Mortimer (Syd) Golden, M.D.

You get the picture. I have an idea to save litigants thousands of dollars in experts' fees. Why not allow the lawyers to write the reports for both sides? I can do it easily. I would muster the best talents of each of these usual suspect experts, and I would conscientiously prepare both reports under a different *nom de plume*. And my fee for both would be a lot less than what each currently charges for one report.

And of course, these reports would be 100% objective as I would sign two of those mandatory forms, certifying that I am unbiased and neutral. How's that for justice?

And, oh yes, back to that frigid Canadian winter day, I did favourably settle my slip-and-fall matter.

But are witnesses always honest? This is as good a time as any to discuss honesty and deception.

CHAPTER TWENTY

Truth Be Told about the Truth

"You can't handle the truth!"
~ Col. Nathan Jessup (Jack Nicholson), from the film *A Few Good Men*

Col. Jessup bellowed these words to Lt. Daniel Kaffee (Tom Cruise) during Kaffee's intense cross-examination. After watching the movie again recently and hearing the line anew, I started thinking about truth and honesty. I noticed there is a myriad of expressions surrounding these concepts. For starters, children use a cute phrase when they feel they have been deceived. I recall once promising to take my then-young son Gabriel to a hockey game. Unfortunately, something urgent came up and I had to cancel. Gabriel was very understanding. He exclaimed, "Liar, liar, pants on fire!"

Although I did not share his assessment of my integrity, Gabriel's comment got me pondering. Perhaps adults should be as explicit and candid as children when confronting dishonesty. It would be refreshing; for example, for a judge to comment in his or her reasons, "I totally reject the defendant's evidence. Liar, liar, pants on fire!" At worst it would get the defendant to look at his pants. And if his pants were consumed by fire, he might now be in a position to tell the "naked truth."

People do not like to be called out for being dishonest. Consider that ubiquitous Wild West movie's saloon-poker scene in which some Johnny Ringo pulls four aces. This does not sit well with some Colorado Kid who is also holding an ace. When the Kid simply clears his throat, Ringo says, "You callin' me a cheater?" If the Kid even blinks, they're both out on the street pronto, a quick gunfight away from Boot Hill. (European version: Gaming room in Paris. The outraged Count Montiago in the midst of playing baccarat slaps the face of the insulting Baron de Grenoble with his glove, challenging him to a duel at dawn. Weapons to be chosen then.)

People are forever trying fervently to convince others that they are honest. A common plea is, "I swear on a stack of bibles." Swearing on even one bible is a very solemn occasion. But which nefarious place can you possibly be banished to if you lie after swearing on a stack of bibles? The Bates Motel?

Then there is the guy who "swears up and down." I imagine this clown in front of a judge and jury, taking a bible into his hands, and uttering the oath while doing five deep squats. Now, who can discredit this individual?

And we have the philosopher. When challenged, he'll say, "Why would I lie?"

Maybe because he can't handle the truth. Not even "a grain of truth."

Let us not forget the people who are so convinced of their honesty that they invite disaster to be visited upon themselves if they are lying. They say, "Cross my heart and hope to die." Some are more specific as to their choice of death: "May I be struck by a bolt of lightning." I believe these people must be taken seriously. I have yet to be in a courtroom and see a bolt of lightning head straight for the witness box. They are bolder than the chickens who direct the consequences of their dishonesty to others. I am talking about the witness who says, "I swear on my children."

Others are really bold and even weird with someone else's children, or even pets, if they are called out for some indiscretion. They'll say, "It's true" or "I'll be a monkey's uncle." I generally suspect these people's integrity.

They likely engage in "monkey business." Some folks view honesty from different elevations. They may be "on the level." Others may be even more honest, on a higher level, being "aboveboard." I actually respect these people as they are likely transparent, "putting their cards on the table."

Then we have the sports-minded people. "He is as straight as an arrow." This one sometimes makes me uneasy. If arrows were as straight as some of these "straight shooters" claim they are, if I were William Tell's son, there is no way I would stand there with that apple on my head.

This topic makes me think of Robert Ripley. How could he have sounded credible in a witness box? Which judge would have bought any of his evidence?

Court Registrar: "Sir, state your name."

Ripley: "Robert Ripley, believe it or not."

Judge (rolling his eyes): "Right!"

And let us not forget the son of all big liars: Pinocchio. I would say the invention of the century (next to the stickie note), would be a fairy that could stand near a witness and ensure his nose grows whenever he lies. It would certainly speed up court trials. It might even put many lawyers out of a job. But that is OK. I mean it. "Scout's honour."

Interestingly, Wikipedia also notes a survey of the most honest occupations. Lawyers? Good guess. But wrong. It's nurses. Who knew? Even with Wiki's endorsement, I doubt most lawyers when they have a nurse to cross-examine would tell the judge, "We have Florence Nightingale in the witness box. It's OK. No questions."

Certainly, nurses may score high on the integrity list. But speaking of nurses, that brings me full circle back to Jack Nicholson. I am reminded of his role as R. P. McMurphy in *One Flew Over the Cuckoo's Nest*. His run-in with Nurse Ratched spooks me. She may have been honest, but I would think twice about crossing her as I would not care to come down with an unexpected lobotomy.

And how prevalent is hanky-panky in the justice system? A law-school professor once told me, "In Canada, lying in court is second only to hockey as our national sport." I can't say. Honestly.

An old proverb reads, "Children and fools tell the truth." Interesting how they have no problem handling it. And how do lawyers try to educe the truth of witnesses? With cross-examination. Sort of similar to what you see in the movies or television. Sort of.

CHAPTER TWENTY-ONE

Cross-Examination: Don't Ask ... Less Is More?

"Were you lying then or are you lying now or
are you a chronic and habitual liar?"
~ Sir Wilfred Robarts (Charles Laughton) from the film *Witness for
the Prosecution*

I s it an art? Is it a science? It's cross-examination! I can say that many law-yers make a mess of it. Certainly, when I was in law school it was never dealt with it. We were taught the substantive law, such as that snail-in-the-ginger-beer case, *Donoghue v. Stephenson*, which revolutionized the law of negligence. But nobody told us what to do when you got the ginger-beer purveyor on the stand for cross-examination. You would have to do better than, "Sir, I suggest to you that you were negligent." A real knockout punch, no doubt. I don't see the jury gasping and saying to themselves, "We've heard enough. Hang Stephenson."

The closest we got to observing a great cross-examination was in the movies. No doubt we all recall the iconic film *Witness for the Prosecution*, where Charles Laughton plays the role of Sir Wilfred Robarts, eminent barrister, who defends Leonard Vole (Tyrone Power). Sir Wilfred conducts a brilliant cross-examination of Christine Vole (Marlene Dietrich), the "wife," surprise witness, who testifies for the prosecution, flip flopping on Leonard's alibi. Sir Wilfred in a loud voice bellows, "Were you lying then or are you lying now or are you a chronic and habitual liar?"

The jury finds the defendant not guilty (of course). I should add that Sir Wilfred had another trick up his sleeve, namely the monocle test, where to establish honesty he would extend his monocle, reflecting a light beam on a character's face and observing their reaction. (Maybe you can consider this tactic in your next trial, but I suggest you ask for the judge's green light.)

I am by far not an expert on cross-examination; however, I have a fair idea of what does not work. Firstly, there are those questions preceded by useless verbiage lawyers often use, such as, "Isn't it a fact that ...?" "Isn't it a fact that you like to binge on wine?"

An alternative version of this piercing question is, "Do you agree that you like to binge on wine?" For some reason, the lawyer believes that "You like to binge on wine?" will elicit a "No" answer and the emphatic setup words "isn't it a fact that" will result in a "yes." Some lawyers don't let go, firing another blank, such as, "Do you expect the court to believe that ...?" I have yet to see a case, where the witness responds, "Actually, I don't expect the court to believe that." Then there are lawyers who believe adding their own verbal reactions will buttress their cross. You'll hear something like,

Lawyer: You threatened Mr. Henderson, did you not?"

Witness: No, I did not.

Lawyer: I see. Hmmm.

An alternative, more assertive reaction is:

Lawyer: Ho, ho. Right!

I doubt this method will result in colleagues beating a path to the lawyer's door, beseeching him to chair the next symposium on effective cross-examinations. And we are all familiar with the caveat, "Never ask a question to which you do not know the answer."

Do any lawyers overlook this admonition? I witnessed a dangerous-driving trial once where the police officer who had followed the defendant who was driving erratically for a distance, confined most of his testimony to the last few seconds before the accident. The defence lawyer in cross-examination asked the officer if his client's driving was OK earlier along the way. The officer looked at his notes and emitting a grin like the Cheshire Cat said, "Actually, now that you mention it …"

Then we have the lawyers who insist on scoring a grand-slam impeachment. The problem is they often blow the process by not properly setting up or completing the impeachment. I had a case once in an aborted house-sale deal, where my client's testimony in an important area differed from what he had said at his examination for discovery (aka deposition). The opposing counsel's ears perked up, but he ran out of fuel somewhere:

Opposing: Mr. Perlman, now you say you really liked my client's house.

Perlman: Yes sir.

Opposing: And at your previous examination, on pg. 137, question 341, did you not say you did not like the house?

Perlman: I'm not sure about those numbers.

Opposing: Sir, what are you sure about?

He then went off in a different direction, after glancing at the judge and smiling smugly. He no doubt thought the judge was thinking, "Sir Wilfred himself."

And I did mention one of my first trials involving that two-seater hovercraft that suffered the fate of the Titanic on its maiden voyage on a lake in Ontario—the case with that impressive expert witness who was involved in designing the hovercraft. This expert was both a marine architect and an aeronautical engineer, the guy with the navy-blue blazer bearing a crest of a colourful hot-air balloon hovering over a mini-submarine.

Fortunately, what saved the day was my very professional near-panic state, where I chose to totally limit my cross-examination of this one man who was a cross between Neil Armstrong and Sir Francis Drake. At that time, I had not yet seen *Witness for the Prosecution*. But even if I had, I doubt I would have asked the judge for leave to perform that monocle test. Thinking back, I believe even Sir Wilfred Robarts would have left this guy alone.

CHAPTER TWENTY-TWO

The Selfies: Do It Yourself (DYI) Lawyer

"A man who is his own lawyer has a fool for a client."
~ Abraham Lincoln

Do-it-yourself lawyer? But are all the self-reps, aka "pro ses," inundating our courts, fools? Many simply cannot afford lawyered access to justice. Nonetheless they create problems for the justice system, as in addition to not knowing the ropes, they lack objectivity, often allowing emotions to run wild.

I recall a cruelty divorce case where my client's husband, Chuck, a bit volatile, fired his lawyer. During a court session (one of several as Chuck wasn't behaving), while in the hallway I asked the gentleman a question about his financial statement. This did not sit too well with Chuck and he lunged at me, shouting, "That's none of your business." (Actually, he did have a graphic adjective describing said business. Elaboration not necessary.) Fortunately, security was nearby. But it was upsetting and obviously memorable.

We lawyers, however, are expected to play by the rules, to act civilly. As Shakespeare said, "Strive mightily but eat and drink as friends." I can say that indeed this wisdom worked for me, even in the most acrimonious matrimonial cases resolving disputes over coffee and bagels. I got the feeling, however, that Shakespeare's strategy might not exactly have worked with Chuck. I sensed that this suggestion would have led Chuck to tell me where to stuff those bagels.

In another matter I wrote to the husband something like, "Hi Bill. Martha retained me to try to amicably resolve this matter with you." I was non-judgmental and polite. Mahatma Gandhi could not have sounded more conciliatory. However, self-represented parties often view their spouse's lawyer with daggers in their eyes. He emailed me unleashing a tirade, saying something like, "Don't call me Bill. You don't even know me. This mess is all my wife's fault, that vixen. You should know better than to be her lawyer. See you in court." At least Bill wasn't violent. Still, I got the feeling I had best not suggest the bagel route.

Judges often cut self-reps slack they would not accord lawyers. I once witnessed a woman hand a document to the judge. She hand wrote the words on the page in a circular spiral layout, like a snake coiled up. To read the document the judge had to turn it around and around like a steering wheel. When questioned by the judge, the lady said, I'm just a poor artist. Unlike my rich husband, I cannot afford a lawyer. Alas." Not surprisingly the judge was patient. I dare any lawyers to try that stunt. If so, the lawyer had better tender that document to the judge pinned onto a Lazy Susan.

My first contact with self-reps was during my early weeks as an articling student when a judge cajoled me into assisting one. I was sitting quietly in the body of the Small Claims Court simply watching. The judge was a colourful elderly lady fondly known as "Ma Henderson." She had a penchant for moving cases through efficiently, sometimes in an unorthodox manner. She loved to see parties arriving with lawyers, or at least law students, and she usually urged litigants to retain one.

One case involved a self-rep calling himself something like "Norman the Upholstery Doctor." He was defending a claim where the plaintiff, one Edna, insisted that he had returned to her a different chair from the one of great sentimental value that she had entrusted to him. During the plaintiff's testimony, he would jump up and shout, "Edna, you know that's a lie."

The judge, after admonishing him repeatedly, suggested she adjourn to enable him to get legal advice. She said to him, "If you were sitting in your den watching hockey and one of your eyeballs popped out, would you try to put it back yourself?" Norman agreed that he would not attempt the fix *pro se*. (To me, this was totally understandable as he was an upholstery doctor, not an ophthalmologist.)

Ma Henderson then suddenly set her sights on me, minding my own business. (This business was definitely different from the one I was minding with Chuck.) Her Honour said, "You look like a law student." I confessed, noting I was "just observing," and she said, "I'm holding this case down. Can you give this man some basic trial advice?"

Given my assumed vast trial experience, I accepted the honour, but with trepidation. Fortunately, I managed to calm the "doctor" down. He seemed to like me and proceeded to hand me his business card. But I will admit that my mind was more focused on that straying eyeball.

This incident happened over forty years ago. I still visualize it. I don't know what ever happened to that business card. I also add that I since had to reupholster my lovely study recliner. However, I thought it best not to chance it by engaging Norman. I did not want to risk my recliner ending up in his shop's Bermuda Triangle.

Many lawyers also provide unbundling services, doing some work, but showing the clients how to perform other tasks themselves. Does it work? Though well-intentioned, unbundling always raised potential malpractice red flags with me. Would a surgeon hand a scalpel to a patient and say, "Appendectomy is a piece of cake. We're now a team. Let me know how it works out. And oh yes—do remember to first wash your hands."

Unlike many other callings, a legal action can be complex and lengthy. The public's exposure to justice is generally what they learn from watching lawyer flicks. After all, all you have to do in a courtroom is talk. Most people are good at this, often not knowing when to stop.

Everybody should have access to justice; however, we lawyers should appreciate it when both sides are lawyered up. Then we can indeed follow Shakespeare's advice. I like my bagels with sesame seeds, toasted, with orange marmalade.

And speaking of good things like orange marmalade, this is a good time as any to ask the question, is the law broke? Need fixin'? Or ain't broke?

CHAPTER TWENTY-THREE

Doing Justice to the Justice System—Is It Broke?

"In the Halls of Justice the only justice is in the halls."

~ Lenny Bruce

G iven the trouble he often got into, the iconic comedian Lenny Bruce certainly was familiar with the halls of justice. Although there are issues all around, I would say there are more problems on the civil side of the justice system than the criminal side. Common gripes are that it is adversarial, not affordable, and above all, it takes years to get your day in court. Is this anything new?

When I started my civil litigation practice in the 1970s, the complaints were similar. I would tell clients my hourly rate was $50, and some would hem and haw. I noted that inflation was high, citing the examples of having to pay $3,000 for my new first car, a Plymouth Duster, 50 cents for a gallon of gas and a recent increase to 19 cents for a single scoop of Baskin-Robbins ice cream. They still hemmed and hawed.

As for court delays, the 1970s here had not yet readily seen pre-trial/ resolution conferences or alternative dispute resolution processes such as mediation. Many more cases went to trial. As I mentioned earlier, at my initial meeting on a personal injury case I would point out the window to an old maple tree saying to my client, "Those leaves will fall off and regrow a few times before your case ever gets to trial."

I now realize it may have rattled them a bit as my own patience is quite finite. I get annoyed when I bring home a rock-hard avocado and I have to wait three to four days for it to ripen.

The problems presumably do not relate to solicitor's corporate/commercial work. I have yet to see a client saying, "I needed a will. I had to wait three days to see my lawyer and another week or so until it was completed. The justice system is in shambles."

Are we too litigious? Too many lawyers? Ontario with a population of over 14 million has about 55,000 lawyers. That's one lawyer for every 254.5 people. (I guess two of those halves with a similar issue have to get together and see the same lawyer.)

Another problem is the frivolous case. Looking south of our Canadian border hardly a week goes by without some weird lawsuit hitting the news. Some of them involve high-profile celebrities. This opus is not about weird cases; however, the following recent legal action bears discussion as it is emblematic of what is thrown into our courts, thereby consuming their resources.

Is the legal system going gaga over Lady Gaga? Jennifer McBride started a legal action against the singer for the $500,000 reward she offered to anybody who safely returned her French bulldogs, Koji and Gustav, that were kidnapped by a handful of thugs during a violent gunpoint robbery a couple of years ago on a Los Angeles street. These guys were eventually arrested and sentenced to jail terms of multiple years.

Lady Gaga posted the reward offer noting that she was heartbroken and that the $500k would be paid "no questions asked." The little problem is that McBride was implicated in the robbery and eventually pleaded no contest to a charge of possession of stolen property, i.e., Koji and Gustav.

Ah huh you say! Chutzpah? (Aka "effrontery," "nerve," or "cheek" for those not familiar with this Yiddish term.)

A California Judge in the summer of 2023 dismissed McBride's claim noting that one cannot profit from their crimes. (That's one for the law.) Offhand, McBride's case looked like a dog's breakfast. However, presumably her lawyer felt comfortable about the legal action. Then again, I would say he likely remained somewhat suspicious about his client. Watch out for red flags, such as her asking, "Sir, any idea who owns that French poodle out there in the hallway?"

And we are not talking only of suing for the reward. The claim in the Superior Court alleged breach of contract, fraudulent misrepresentation, and so on, and even included a claim for damages for mental distress and loss of enjoyment of life. I'm sure we can all understand the part about the loss of enjoyment of life. After all, $500,000 can buy you a fair bit of enjoyment. You can even go out and purchase a couple of pure-breed French bulldogs.

The legal question thrown at the court was "is there a breach of contract?" After all, there was an offer and an acceptance. Doesn't this sound similar to that iconic *Carlill v. Carbolic Smoke Ball* case back in England in 1893 where the smoke ball company offered €100 to anyone who used their product and still contracted the flu? The court found for the plaintiff, Lilli Carlill, noting that the defendant's advertisement constituted an enforceable contract and was not mere puffery. (I guess that's what the British called it in 1893.) Then again, this Gaga dogs' case in my view is similar in principle. I would say it is on all fours with the Smoke Ball.

Does it matter that there was something shady about the McBride's connection to the robbers? You might then ask if it would have made a difference if Lilli Carlill had come down with the flu had she used a stolen smoke ball. Then again, who in their right mind would steal a smoke ball? Also, the thieves tried to nab three French bulldogs but succeeded in nabbing only Koji and Gustav. A third one, Asia, escaped. The police eventually located Asia. My question is, would the police officers also be entitled to this reward? After all, the reward offer is unconditional. I have no information that the cops also lined up for that reward.

McBride's lawyer certainly had some interesting work cut out for him in this legal action. For example, the trial could have been interesting. I can just visualize McBride's lawyer with his opening questions as he establishes her background for the jury:

McBride's lawyer: "Ms. McBride, as for your occupation, I understand you are a fence."

Hey, better it comes out right at the beginning.

The result in the case did not surprise me. Certainly, McBride was the underdog. I would not have expected it to settle out of court. I doubt Lady Gaga would have paid McBride any cash. I would have suggested a win-win resolution. Lady Gaga could have offered to do a benefits concert at the jail where McBride's accomplices are guests. Sounds good? This resolution would certainly have helped free up some of the court's limited resources.

Fortunately, not all jurisdictions are consumed with litigious matters, running to the courts to deal with them. Japan for example, with a population of over 126 million has approximately 40,000 lawyers. That's one lawyer or "bengoshi" for every 3,150 people. Even I cannot speculate why this is but from my deep research (Wikipedia), it seems there is a cultural aversion in Japan to lawsuits. Historically, Japanese customs instituted an avoidance of legal involvement as it disrupted harmony. I can attest to this theory as I got sued once and when served with the claim, it certainly disrupted my previous harmonious state.

There are numerous actions that in my view should not happen as they impact the court resources big time. I recall reading about that case where a customer sued a dry cleaner in Washington for $54,000,000 following the disappearance of his pair of pants. Fortunately for the dry cleaner, the action was dismissed. But I am sure the case must have thrown off his harmony. Here we had a litigant who tried to take a cleaner to the cleaners.

I note that Japan has over 60,000 people over the age of 100. Many reside in the fishing villages of Okinawa. Could it be that many lawyers or would-be lawyers decide on foregoing a legal career for a shot at longevity, opting for a career of catching mahi-mahi? I will admit that while in practice this theory never crossed my mind.

Speaking of longevity, what are some of the notable causes of delays in getting a case to trial? Shortage of judges? Lack of court space? Maybe. How about procedural hurdles? One is the jury system for civil cases. Eats up time, big time. Good thing they don't have juries in the medical world telling doctors what to do. I would sooner see doctors resorting to leeches.

Then there are other time-consuming procedural wrangles. I am not talking about the court registrar opening the session bellowing, "Oyez, oyez, oyez." For example, I am not sure the public is impressed with displays of pomp and tradition such as judges and lawyers wearing robes or wigs. Nor would it help much if they cut it down to one oyez. I am talking about the lengthy delays suffered in moving a case forward given the rules of discovery, production of documents, and so on. You just hope opposing counsel will comply with the rules and disclose. But if they decide to play hardball, the adversarial element rears its nasty head and the parties become more polarized. Which gets me back to Japan.

There is no automatic right there to disclosure. If you really need some information, you have to ask the court to order the opponent to disclose it. However, it might be awkward to ask for something you don't know exists. Of interest also is that there is no provision for the courts to award the successful side legal costs. This gap in jurisdiction might certainly discourage that fishing expedition (the proverbial one, not the one for mahi-mahi).

Is anything better? With COVID-19 we have seen the courts resorting to virtual hearings. Of course, there have been hitches and glitches, such as images freezing; voices going mute; and occasionally, the background image of the ornate courtroom giving way to a glimpse of the judge's real background.

I suppose, given that everyone was likely at home, they could be a bit discretionary about their attire, especially if they were behind a desk. It reminds me of that Groucho Marx comment in the movie *Duck Soup*, where he discusses military strategies, saying, "Dig the trenches big enough, the soldiers won't need pants." That is almost a line that dry cleaner might have used in defense of that lawsuit. I do not recommend during a virtual hearing that anybody ever ask a judge for disclosure about that one.

Will increased use of technology help the situation? It is a good start. Or is it? I am talking about the frustrations we all face daily trying to navigate through a technological jungle when we call a bank, insurance company, or most other mega corporations. I would say the law as it stands offers no protection or solace. I am talking about welcome to "your call is important to us."

Thank you for holding … and holding

There are three certainties in life: death, taxes, and the impossibility of getting through on the telephone to a mammoth outfit like a bank within a reasonable time. Since there is not much more we can do about death or taxes, let me wail about those banks. Actually, I am not certain we can do much about them either. But there ought to be some laws to compensate consumer victims for the hassles we must daily endure.

I recently received a statement regarding a credit card I never use. I applied for that card as one perk was bags fly free on an airline that I also never use. For that matter, for years I had not used the bank issuing this card. The statement had a charge for $1,175 allegedly incurred by me in Moose Jaw, Saskatchewan, for something like the Antler Motel. As I have never had the pleasure of visiting Saskatchewan, I called the bank. Presumably whoever did run it up either spent a few nights there or maybe one or two supposedly in their Royal Suite.

Given the apparent gravity, I expected to get through to the right bank department within minutes. Then again, the Blue Jays probably expected to win the World Series last season. The recording prompted me to hit 7 to report unrecognized charges. It continued with, "We are experiencing more call volume than usual. Wait times might be longer." I wonder about this caveat. When was it ever usual? In 1897?

What then followed was about an hour of unrelenting, annoying, and repetitive music. The best of Mick Jagger shouting would have been preferable. This ordeal was interrupted sporadically by a comment like, "Did you know you can visit us online, where you can also review our privacy policy?" Just what I wanted to check out. No doubt that Moose Jaw knave reviewed their privacy policy and got ideas.

I decided to call again from my mobile phone this time and opt for the stolen card department, while keeping my place for the fraud department open on my landline. After a half hour I reached a live agent called Marlene. She told me she could take some information, but I should still maintain my call to the fraud department. Firstly, she had to ask me some verifying questions. My date of birth. I passed this one with flying colours. Next, she asked how many accounts I had with this bank. I likely had a dormant account. I guessed one. Pass.

Then came the kicker, "When did you last use it?" I had no clue, other than that's why it was dormant. I said, "ages ago." She replied, "The system does not accept this answer. You are locked out." Marlene did apologize, adding that she lives in Vancouver, but she also had never visited Moose Jaw. At least we had rapport. But this did not satisfy the system.

I continued to wait for almost three hours in total until another live person from fraud came on. Hello, John from Moncton New Brunswick. He asked whether I incurred those charges. I told him I did not though I had heard good things about that Antler Motel. After a brief post-midnight chat, he noted the debit would be removed. Two days later I received a survey asking how I enjoyed this experience. I was asked to rate on a scale of 1 to 10 factors, such as how soon it took to reach an agent and would I recommend this bank to my friends. Who ever said banks don't have a sense of humour?

We cannot do much more about death or taxes. Can we do something about trying to get through to banks or for that matter other behemoth organizations such as insurance and utility companies? Keeping customers on the line endlessly, adding insult to injury with annoying music, and robotic lame excuses is abusive.

What to do? This is a universal problem. I urge governments to set up a damages system similar to workers' compensation legislation. Create a consumer reparations chart making the culprits pay for their inane comments and actions, as follows:

1. Your call is important to us: $1,000.

2. We are experiencing more calls than usual: $2,000.

3. We are experiencing more calls than usual; if call is around 3 A.M: $5,000.

4. Did you know you can get all your questions answered by visiting us online: $7,500 if the institution actually does have live people working there. $10,000 if it has a robot from Edmonton called Gerald.

5. This call may be recorded to serve you better: $12,000 … minimum.

6. We can call you back. You will not lose your place in the queue. $1,000 per day after they get back to you around Easter as you did lose your place in the queue.

7. After your call goes nowhere, agent says to you, "How else can I help you? $13,000 plus damages for injuries suffered busting your gut laughing.

8. Bombarding the customer with harassing music: $1,000 per tune. $20,000 if there is only one relentless tune.

9. Message asks you to complete a survey as company actually takes surveys seriously: $10,000 plus give the CEO 25 lashes.

10. While talking to an agent you get cut off and they never call you back saying, "Our system does not enable callbacks": Hey, ever hear of a telephone? Just force these guys to install a normal telephone. Even a dial phone should work.

I am sure that had Alexander Graham Bell known customer service would get to this, he would never have invented the telephone. I actually invite comments to my suggestions. I do take these matters seriously.

And so, is the system broke? It ain't perfect. But as my favourite philosopher Yogi Berra said, "If the world were perfect, it wouldn't be." And speaking of fixing, the legal profession is known to be a bit conservative—not often in the forefront of change. I'm sure we are all curious about what Sir Winston Churchill said about change.

CHAPTER TWENTY-FOUR

Hold the Change—How Conservative Is the Legal Profession?

"To improve is to change; to be perfect is to change often."
~ Sir Winston Churchill

This is as fine an hour as any to quote the statesman, and talk about change. Given the law profession is a bit conservative, I suppose lawyers are not perfect. I was generally ambivalent about change. I thought we had it all with the arrival of the stickie note.

I think of the Commissioner of the United Statutes Patent Office from 1898 to 1901, Charles Holland Duell, who allegedly said, "Everything that can be invented has been invented." Duell would probably have given the Wright brothers a tough time: "Ahem. Flight has already been invented. Those other brothers, the Montgolfiers, came up with the hot-air balloon. They successfully sent up a sheep, a duck, and a chicken. What more can your "invention" supposedly achieve?"

I wouldn't trust this guy to read my palm. Incidentally, Duell eventually became an appeals judge in Washington D.C. I doubt he rendered many dissents.

Changes usually come with a flip side. Say the telephone. During the 1970s/80s BC (before cellphones), the trial judge would announce a recess. This announcement was more like the sound of a racing starter's pistol. The lawyers would scramble out to the nearby handful of pay phones. We just had to call our offices to see what the next crisis was. And there were always more lawyers than pay phones. Like musical chairs. And you needed those precious dimes. My main benefactor of dimes was Millie, the courthouse coffee-shop cashier. With a smile she had the coveted dimes in her hand as she saw me approaching. There were some cashiers, like Clarence, who would snap at the lawyers saying, "Am I the Royal Bank?"

Being in Millie's good books was almost as important as landing the right judge. Before court I would diligently check out who was sitting today at the cash register.

Eventually the cellphone arrived. Shangri-la? The problem now is many of us cannot tear ourselves away from our cellphones. There is this millennial lawyer, Sidney, in my neighbourhood who walks his beagle, always chatting on his phone (Sidney, not the beagle). He's completely oblivious to his surroundings, bellowing remarks such as, "Fifty grand is a good start," or "Never mind what your surveillance shows. You caught my client on a good day." I'm sure the beagle feels neglected. I haven't seen it but it would not surprise me if after doing his business on the sidewalk, the hound would whip out a plastic bag and pick up the goods himself.

And speaking of goods, I think of our Toronto Great Library, built in the 1800s. For decades and into the 1970s/80s BC (before computers), often when a reported case was successfully appealed, some lawyers would anonymously open the volume containing the trial decision and pencil in something like, "Appeal allowed: February 21, 1973." This act of kindness saved other lawyers from relying on this now-overturned decision. I sometimes wondered whether this news dissemination system was open to sabotage. I suppose such saboteurs would be the precursors of today's trolls. Unfortunately, trolls have not changed.

I will admit I prefer online case research to the work of these pencil phantoms, which brings me to social media. I think it is often overused or misused. I do not get excited when I read of some lawyer's LinkedIn post announcing, "I am listening to a podcast next Monday afternoon from my deputy mayor about our pothole crises in Belleville." Thanx for telling me. I was going to catch an online webinar on trial tactics but now I have a scheduling conflict. Which brings me to the Zooms. Thanx to COVID-19, Zoom and similar programs have become a communication lifeline for our profession, enabling legal education and the justice system to function safely. Though I find it fascinating, as a boomer I am relieved that I never had to practise law this way.

These days, since my retirement from practice I tune in to some events such as exercises or lectures, or try to but often get sidelined with technical glitches. Too often I see a notice saying that the host is letting me in, but he doesn't. I then have to scramble and call some 800 tech support number in Atlanta. A voicemail answers telling me I can probably easily solve my issue by going online. Right. I would sooner spend my time fixing those potholes in Belleville.

I also would not feel confident whether or not opposing counsel could coach his client a bit during an examination to make sure he gives the right answer. Of course, most of us are above board, but then again, with advanced technology it may not be long before our keyboards have a function such as, "control-kick client."

I do consider change inevitable, but no one dose fits all, especially with technology. Do some changes go over the top? Though Churchill says being perfect is to change often, I agree more with that sage comment of Yogi Berra, where he said, "If the world were perfect, it wouldn't be." Actually, I often use this Yogi quote in my writings. That's fine. I see no reasons for this practice to change.

Now for a personal revelation: Have I ever mentioned I am a proud practising technophobe?

CHAPTER TWENTY-FIVE

Boomer Technophobia—Yikes!

"One of the biggest risks to the future of civilization is AI."
~ Elon Musk

G reat minds do think alike. Technophobia greatly impacted my work-ing life. I resisted change because I was both a boomer and a member of a very conservative profession. When I was called to the Bar in 1974 B.C. (Before Computers), the local courthouse library even still carried a book called *Oliphant on the Law of Horses*, 1908 edition. I doubt there was a long borrowing waitlist. And I really doubt if you missed the due return date you'd get a nasty call from the librarian saying something like, "Hey, how selfish can you be?"

I was the youngest in a space-sharing arrangement. The mainstay office tool then was the typewriter. If your assistant made an error, she (probably 99% of assistants then were "she") would dab some liquid white-out onto the paper, wait for it to dry, and then type the correct characters. Whiteout was our delete function.

Then along came the magic invention: the IBM Selectric type-writer with auto correction. If you made a typo, you just backspaced and hit a correcting button, triggering an erasing ribbon to delete the letters *non grata*. This awesome device likely rivalled the invention of the Gutenberg press.

I was the first lawyer there, as expected, to get one of these amazing machines. The cost then was about $1,000. That was a lot of money in those days for a device where you exclaim, "Hey Siri" and nothing happens.

I recall the day the IBM guy delivered and demonstrated the machine. The entire office gathered around. The scene looked like that historic moment in 1903 at Kitty Hawk. "Orville Wright" deliberately misspelled "banana," adding an extra *n*. With a devilish smile, he back tracked, magically deleted the word, and retyped it without the offensive extra *n*. Everyone in the room uttered a loud "aah."

The oldest lawyer there, Simon, was very skeptical, suspiciously observing the IBM guy. I waited for Simon to leave and return with some firewood and shout, "Don't believe it. It's a trick. He's a witch."

Computers did not start inundating law offices until the mid-1980s. The lawyers would hover around our assistants watching with awe how they moved words around or redid pages of script in seconds. There was no internet then. If you wanted to look up a word, you opened the *Oxford Dictionary* or *Roget's Thesaurus* to find a suitable synonym or antonym. I was comfortable with that. In fact, I still have my dog-eared copy of *Roget's Thesaurus*, which I bought for 35 cents in 1959.

Then came the end of the century. Remember Y2K, where the doomsayers predicted all our computers would go bananas (spelled properly the first attempt)? I started finding practising progressively more frustrating because of lightning-speed technology changes.

One of the rages became the paperless office. Not for this boomer. Although I see advantages of having quick access to reams of information, I like to have a document I can touch and spread on my desk and read, scribbling pencil notes, and making highlights with a yellow highlighter.

As well, I was simply not able to fathom paying $2,500 for a medical legal report and then shredding it. Blasphemy!

I found that the tech issues created a new dimension of dependence on an unlikely but not unusual source: our children. I found myself calling my kids for support on everything from what a browser was to how to clear a cache. And what a cache was. My son Daniel, an insurance lawyer, incidentally, once planned a visit to New York. I graciously lent him my paper map. He demonstrated his appreciation by unfolding it and saying facetiously: "I am pressing my finger on 42nd Street. How come I am not getting a Google Street View?" He went on to graciously decline my generous offer of the marked-up and colourful yellow-highlighted map that had served me well. Incidentally, I reviewed my will afterwards to make sure I wasn't leaving him my *Roget's*.

My final years of practice saw the evolution of e-filing, e-discovery, e-this, and e-that. I recall attending a conference whereby a young trial lawyer noted that when he conducts a jury trial, he has all the proposed evidence on a computer, demonstrating it on a projector. In court, he hands out iPads to opposing counsel, the judge, the witness, the court registrar, and the jury members. I was knocked off my feet. I did, however, say to myself that likely the expense for all these iPads was probably less than the cost of my IBM Selectric. The kid was adamant that anyone not practising this way was in the horse-and-buggy age. I mentioned this to my smart-ass son, and he asked me who my blacksmith was. (I guess he won't be on the lookout for a copy of *Oliphant on Horses*.)

Even filing my annual errors-and-omissions insurance application had to be done online. I was always concerned if, while fumbling through it, I made errors or omissions. Not a good impression. We lawyers are not the quickest group to adapt to change. And the boomers likely land well off the middle of the bell curve on this one. This is a different bell from the telephone system companies. Though tempted, I will not go there, other than to say that when push-button phones came into being and we would get a voice that said: "And if you have a dial phone, please stay on the line," I stayed on the line. At least that led to dealing with a live person.

No doubt the COVID necessitated tech changes such as virtual trials, electronic filing, and other innovations made mandatory after COVID hit would have knocked me out of the bell. Not for me. As for Zoom, no thanx. In over four decades of court hearings, I never got caught with my pants down (literally at least).

Since I am venting about technology, why not vent about another peeve I have: the corporation?

CHAPTER TWENTY-SIX

The Corporation—Neither a Soul to Be Damned nor an Ass to Be Kicked

"Just one more thing ... There's something that bothers me."

~ Columbo

I shall start off by quoting Shakespeare: "Fie on the company!" Well, to be accurate, the bard did say the fie part.

Now retired from practice, I am reflecting on what about the legal system bugs me. High on the list is the concept that a company has its own independent status. I see no reason why there should be a corporate veil protecting a company's owners from personal liability.

There is rhyme and reason to my opinion. My first concept of a corporation dates back to childhood, shopping with my mother at Steinberg's, a now defunct chain supermarket in Montreal. Steinberg's used to issue trading stamps called "Pinky," redeemable for gifts. During one visit my mother got into a dispute with the cashier about the number of Pinky stamps we should get for our purchase. We all got a bit vocal, and the store manager was summoned. I recall butting in and asking him to call over Mr. Steinberg. He looked at us smugly and said, "This has nothing to do with Mr. Steinberg. It's company policy."

This experience soured my concept of corporate status. Why should the real owner wiggle out of responsibility? My mom and I were tempted to barge through that "employees only" door where we were sure Mr. Steinberg was comfortably settled counting his profits (and likely his Pinky stamps). We expected him, as owner, to resolve the issue with us. We left disgruntled.

I now think of a comment by the eighteenth-century Lord Chancellor, Edward, First Baron Thurlow, who said, "Did you ever expect a corporation to have a conscience when it has no soul to damn and no body to kick?"

That day while arguing with the manager, my mom and I certainly would have liked to have Mr. Steinberg in front of us, thereby giving us the option to consider doing what the Lord Chancellor said cannot be done to a company.

I now think about that scene in Shakespeare's *Julius Caesar* where after Caesar's assassination an angry mob descends upon the streets of Rome looking for the conspirators. One of the conspirators is a politician, Cinna. While the lynch mob is out hunting for the culprits, they come across a different Cinna, namely Cinna the poet. Unfortunately for this Cinna, the collective finds the name match is good enough to constitute guilt. Quoting:

Third Citizen

Your name, sir, truly.

Cinna the Poet

Truly, my name is Cinna.

First Citizen

Tear him to pieces; he's a conspirator.

Cinna the Poet

I am Cinna the poet, I am Cinna the poet.

Fourth Citizen

Tear him for his bad verses, tear him for his bad verses.

Cinna the Poet

I am not Cinna the conspirator.

Fourth Citizen

It is no matter, his name's Cinna; pluck but his name out of his heart and turn him going.

To my mom and me, Mr. Steinberg and Steinberg's was close enough. No doubt, however, we would have been much kinder to Mr. Steinberg. All we wanted was what was owing to us, namely those short-changed Pinky stamps.

The landmark case of *Salomon v. Salomon*, decided in 1895 by the House of Lords, affirmed this unjust and egregious corporate immunity principle. Creditors sued the company's principles for its debts. However, the court unanimously held that the company was an independent person with its rights and liabilities of itself, and that "the motives of those who took part in the promotion of the company are absolutely irrelevant in discussing what those rights and liabilities are."

Thus, the legal fiction of "corporate veil" between the company and its owners was firmly created by the Salomon case. As Shakespeare might say, "Fie on the creditors." The fallout of this ridiculous ruling has resulted in inestimable losses and damage to good people. It cost us a few well-deserved Pinky stamps.

One may ask what the responsibility of owners in large corporations should be. I am talking public companies. I see little difference. All corporations have neither soul to be damned nor a body to be kicked. I say the shareholders should always be responsible. For example, I own a number of Apple shares. This makes me a part owner no doubt. I will say I do not flaunt my ownership status. I recently visited an Apple Store to have my torn iPhone cover replaced. I did not say to the associate something like, "I'm one of your bosses. I'll just help myself to that orange one there."

Yet if anybody were to make a claim against Apple, I consider looking to me as fair ball. I would never think of saying anything like, "Hey. You can't sue me. Uh uh. Remember *Salomon v. Salomon*." I don't have a double standard. My obligation should be proportional to my stake in Apple. And so, if there is some class action resulting in a large judgment, I have no problem receiving a notice from the corporation's lawyer saying, "Sorry, but we got hammered. Please remit the amount of 17 cents." This makes sense to me. I own up to my responsibilities. I'll do an e-transfer right away.

It's been many decades since I had that childhood supermarket experience. Steinberg's is long gone. And we know it did not have a conscience. No company does. However, this simple matter could readily have been resolved satisfactorily had we, as we should have, had an audience with Mr. Steinberg.

I did say I had a rhyme and reason for my views. Aren't we all perhaps influenced at times by life's Pinky stamps? Fie on the company. And speaking of companies, there is one type of company you cannot live with or without. This company hangs around all of us in one way or another, especially if you practise law. I talk of the insurance company.

CHAPTER TWENTY-SEVEN

Yes, We Have No Insurance Coverage Today

**"I detest life-insurance agents: they always argue
that I shall someday die, which is not so."**
~ Stephen Butler Leacock

As lawyers, many of us exercise our access to justice by either fighting insurance companies or defending them. Sue or defend, we are all connected with insurance by buying it. When did insurance start?

It's suggested that insurance originated with Babylonian King Hammurabi around 1750 B.C. He encoded the concept of "bottomry," where a merchant, for a few shekels extra, would not have to repay his creditor's loan unless the ship arrived safely. No idea why it's called bottomry. Given my experiences litigating against insurance companies, it likely related to a coverage exclusion. The merchant whose stuff never arrived would plead with the creditor to forgive the loan and the creditor would balk, saying, "Can you prove your merchandise ended up at the bottom of the sea? Your plea for forgiveness of the loan is hereby denied."

My first experience with insurance was in Montreal when I was about seven. A pesky life-insurance agent, one Jean-Paul, came to our house trying to sell my father a policy. He gained admittance to our house, winning our confidence as he used to send us a calendar annually. My dad, however, grew impatient, telling calendar man to call him in a week. Jean-Paul then uttered a frightening comment, "What if, meanwhile, something should happen to you?"

This ominous comment rattled me. My father laughed, but after explaining it to me, I became even more spooked. I almost expected the shoe to drop. We went to the barber the next day, and I clenched my hands when I saw the barber sharpen his razor. To my delight, the barber only gave my dad's sideburns a good trim. Phew!

My next contact with insurance was in my teens when I applied for a summer job at a large insurance company. The interviewer was an elderly, seasoned insurance gentleman, somewhat resembling Sir Winston Churchill. He told me he saw beauty in insurance, noting, "An airplane can't get off the ground without insurance." He followed up with an uncontrollable belly laugh. I, for some reason, was readily able to contain my laughter. Sir Winston didn't hire me. I guess that interview was not my finest hour. My discomfort with insurance companies was refreshed.

What always impressed me is the opulence of these leviathans. Most downtowns have office towers named after insurance giants. Montreal hosts the century-plus old Sunlife Building, once the largest building in the British Commonwealth. Interestingly, this building secretly housed Britain's gold reserves during WWII after being shipped to Canada in 1940 in crates labelled "fish." This stealth event was called "Operation Fish." (Creative wasn't it!) I wonder if the gold was insured. WWII ends and the gold is missing in action. Churchill sues.

The insurance company claims misrepresentation as the manifest said "kippers." The insurer refuses coverage, saying to Churchill," Your claim sleeps with the fishes." Claim denied. (Good for him for not hiring me.)

Many of my cases in practice involved motor-vehicle accidents, i.e., insurance. For fun I Googled to find out when the first two-car accident happened. I found that in 1895 there were only two cars in Cleveland, and they collided. No clue how. Maybe it would have helped had there been a radio traffic report, allowing each driver to take evasive measures:

Driver Smith: I hear Williams is on Lakeshore Avenue. I'd best wait until he leaves.

Driver Williams: I hope Smith heard that and doesn't come near me with his jalopy.

I don't know how the insurers worked that one out. Presumably, the desks of the respective adjusters were not too cluttered with files.

My practice also included property-damage claims, fire, and theft (not bottomry). Insurers frequently denied fire claims, suggesting the client committed arson. They would conduct an intensive credit investigation, concluding that the insured needed money. Insurers don't require my advice; however, as I am retired, I'll offer it: To securely underpin this arson motive, why don't they just specify it as an exclusion?

"Exclusions: 23g. We do not insure loss or damage caused by fire where the insured directly or indirectly needs, wants, or enjoys money."

This provision should about cover all potential claims.

Claim denied.

What often amazes me is that insurers readily pay out thousands of dollars, no problem, but recoil on nickel-and-dime items. Once, while on a cruise, I developed a medical issue and the good ship's doctor told me to check it out further at a hospital when we dock in China. My travel insurer reimbursed the transportation to the hospital and medical costs but balked at paying the $50 bill for the translator the ship arranged to accompany me. The adjuster insisted my policy did not encompass translators.

On the one hand, his position annoyed me. On the other hand, I was flattered that he thought I could maneuver my way from the port, to and through the hospital administration and examination experience because, no doubt, he presumed I was fluent in Mandarin. The only word or sound that may have come in handy with the doctor would have been "Ah." (I know I did say earlier I learned some Mandarin from my clients. But this was mere puffery.) Fortunately, eventually the insurance honoured it. They appreciated my efforts to access justice.

Given that we drive cars, live in houses, and travel, can a day in our lives pass during which insurance does not have a presence?

As for that life insurance, Jean-Paul never followed up with my father. I don't know why. Maybe something happened to him.

I guess Stephen Leacock did not expect to die. Maybe he is still around, like Elvis. Who knows? And speaking of fiction, let's have a look at fact and fiction in the legal systems, including in the differences between Canadian and American court practices.

CHAPTER TWENTY-EIGHT

Fact and Fiction: It Ain't What You See in the Movies

"Things are seldom what they seem, skim milk masquerades as cream."
~ *HMS Pinafore* by W. S. Gilbert and Arthur Sullivan

Under the Border

There are a number of misconceptions as to what actually happens in a courtroom. These myths are generated by movies and television shows. You see, things are run a little differently in Canada than they are south of the border:

a. Objection

No such animal here in Canadian courts. If the lawyer doesn't like what the other lawyer is saying, generally because he's getting close to the truth, he or she will not say "objection." If he does the judge might say, "What is it, Mr. Ferguson?"

The drill is to stand up. When the judge sees you, he or she will say something like, "Yes, what is it Mr. Ferguson?" The lawyer will then think of something important to say having successfully interrupted his adversary's train of thought and effective cross-examination of the witness. Although we don't use the word objection, it is beyond me why in Canada we have not come up with an alternative word. Something simple. How about "hello"?

b. Order in the court

I have been practising in the Canadian courts for ages and I have never seen a gavel in the courtroom. Yet there is not a caricature of a judge without a gavel in his hand. This again must be an American creation. I don't know what the purpose of a gavel would be in any event. The voice from the bench readily gets heard throughout. It's not as if the courtroom is the size of Yankee Stadium. I guess the reason why the American judges have gavels is security. It may not be a magnum, but I've seen these hammers and a zealous litigant might think twice before lunging at the bench with his fingers.

c. What is a continuance?

Apparently when American lawyers want to postpone or reschedule a hearing they ask for a continuance. Here we ask for an adjournment. This makes more sense to me as you are more specifically asking the court to put the matter over, that is, to adjourn it. It also makes more sense to me because I am more familiar with adjournment than continuance. And remember lawyers are not the fastest innovators. Adjournment for me. Now let me continue.

d. Will counsel approach the bench

Also, no such animal in Canada. People watching from the body of the court might get the idea that the judge is having a private conversation with the lawyers to their respective detriment. Also, I guess one party might have better ears than the other and thereby pick up the private conversation. He could then wink at his less-endowed opponent and all hell might break loose.

In Canadian courts, if the judge wants a private conversation with counsel, he recesses the court and says, "I want to see counsel in my chambers." This then really gives the litigants a good reason to feel something secretive is going on behind their backs and their respective lawyers are trying to sell them out.

e. This comment will be stricken from the record

Another all-American feature. And an amusing one at that. We see a lawyer suggesting to a witness charged with assault something improper and irrelevant like, "And I understand, sir, that you have an automatic firearm collection," and after he cries "Yes!" before the opposing lawyer gets a chance to object, he demands and the judge orders: "This testimony will be stricken from the record. The jury will disregard this evidence."

Like Dorothy said of the Scarecrow, I like this one the most. Here we have twelve people who are given the responsibility of determining whether a person goes free or possibly goes to jail, or worse. Yet the judge expects them to act like morons and willfully forget some of the juiciest testimonies of the trial.

In Canadian courts nothing ever gets stricken from the record. The judge may merely remind the jurors during his final charge to the jury that they should not take this evidence into account. I am sure no Canadian jury would even think of rendering their decision with this tainted evidence when asked to disregard it.

f. The King v. The People

In the United States, the prosecution side of a criminal case is referred to as "The People." In other words, the case will be designated as *The People v. Brown*. In Canada, the people are replaced collectively and substituted by "the King." The Latin designation is usually used, and so the court docket will read, *Rex v. Brown*.

Our prosecutors are even referred to as Crown Attorneys or simply as Crowns. South of the border they're District Attorneys or DAs. I prefer the American system as the Canadian one puts too much pressure on His Majesty the King. For example, if the culprit Mr. Brown decides to shoplift a tumbler of shampoo from a Wal-Mart in Dallas, then it is the people of Texas who will prosecute him. When the culprit Brown sees the docket reading *The People of Texas v. Brown*, he'll no doubt get overwhelmed and this will be the last the courts will see of him. He'll think twice before committing another larceny. All the people of Texas are certainly a massive force to face, more massive than even Wal-Mart. But if he were to do the same thing in Edmonton, it would be Brown against the King. One on one. If he's any sort of chauvinist, I doubt he'll be put off by a septuagenarian gentleman across the ocean waiving his finger at him and saying, "Shame, shame."

Furthermore, prosecuting thousands of charges a year must put a tremendous strain on His Majesty. Imagine the busy schedule he has performing his monarchial duties, like travelling to New Guinea to watch tribal dances or attending state dinners from Ottawa to San Francisco. The last thing he needs is to get a call on his cellular phone from some police officer in Edmonton asking, "Your Majesty, what do you want us to do with Mr. Brown?"

Even if Wal-Mart might want the charges dropped, it is the King himself who is the aggrieved party, the victim so to speak. When that rogue snatched the shampoo from Wal-Mart, little did he know His Majesty King Charles might have to go next door to his wife, Queen Camilla, and say, "Excuse me dear. Can I borrow your Head and Shoulders?" It would therefore only be fair for the loss to be spread among all the people as it is in the United States. Meanwhile, God Save the King. He needs it.

And given that what people see on television and movies about trials is pure fiction, what about the lawyers themselves? I talk of fictional lawyers. They certainly can shape our view of the legal profession. Let me discuss some of my favourites.

Fictional lawyers

As promised, I'll start with one of my major influencers, Perry Mason. After careful analysis I have come to the conclusion that my childhood idol, Perry Mason, probably ended up an obscure bankrupt. How do I arrive at my conclusion you ask? I recently watched another couple of rerun episodes, and I am convinced beyond a reasonable doubt that Perry Mason must have gone belly up unless he supplemented his law practice income by driving a taxi (Uber if it were now).

The telltale signs of a law practice in trouble were obvious in the very first scene of the counselor's office. It was readily apparent that Mason's entire practice consisted of one active case. Can anyone say they ever saw any files on his desk? In fact, the only paper in the office was supplied by his secretary, Della Street, in the form of her steno pad when she was summoned by Perry to record the interview with the unfortunate client. The client would admit it looked bad for her, but insisted she was innocent notwithstanding the fact the police found her fingerprints on the poker that bludgeoned the deceased.

At least his office wasn't too pretentious. I note he didn't even have a swivel chair, making do with a simple low back wooden seat. He was often seen sitting on the front corner of his desk as he chatted with his client. I imagine this was made possible only by the fact that his desk remained uncluttered by files.

I would have expected that legal wiz to be inundated with clients, not because he was invincible but because he never asked his clients for a deposit retainer. I have watched dozens of shows and I am still waiting for him to say, "I'll need five hundred dollars up front." (This was the 1950s, after all.) Maybe if he would have been paid he would have been able to afford a better chair.

But if his lot was so bad, what can we say about the plight of Hamilton Burger, the District Attorney? We don't doubt he got paid, although probably not too much. You will note he always wore that same light gray suit. Then again, to be fair, the episodes were recorded colourless, in black and white. And what a life! We all win some and lose some, but Hamilton never won a case. I have watched him in action carefully trying to analyze his technique in an attempt to account for his dismal record of no wins and about seven thousand losses.

It's amazing what you can get away with working as a civil servant! If he were to display this type of bleak track record in private practice, after three months his partners would have him doing research. Yet, if you think about it, Burger's demeanor readily matched Perry's. His "objection, Your Honor," was just as sound as Perry Mason's, but it was all to no avail. I can only conclude the fault lay not with Hamilton Burger but rather with Lieutenant Tragg, the crusty old detective who accounted for all the arrests on the show.

In view of the fact that Perry Mason got everyone of the defendants off, has anyone ever realized that Tragg must have arrested thousands of innocent people? He has to be history's worst cop. He always arrested the wrong person and then he handed the lemon of a case over to Hamilton Burger who then got tagged for the loss. Sending Burger into court with a Lieutenant Tragg arrest was about as fair as sending Austin Matthews onto the ice without a jock strap.

But still, what made the great Perry Mason tick? One thing I noticed is Della was always in court at his counsel table with her ubiquitous steno pad glued to her hand. Considering Perry only had one client I guess it did not matter what Della was doing. But what happened if she was in court and the phone would ring? This was before the days of the answering machine. Nor did I ever hear an answering service get Mason's line. No wonder he only had one client. He was unreachable!

But the quality that set Perry Mason leagues above other lawyers was his never-ending ability not only to secure acquittals for his clients but also to apprehend the actual murderer. He would do this to the amazement of Lieutenant Tragg and Hamilton Burger.

For some inexplicable reason, as I mentioned earlier, at every murder trial the real murderer always seemed to attend the trial of the innocent accused. He was just asking for it, like the male courting the female spider. Invariably at the end of the episode, investigator Paul Drake walked in, whispered something to Mason and a minute later the murderer stood up in the courtroom and said, "Okay, I did it. It was my poker."

After hundreds of cases Hamilton Burger and Lieutenant Tragg should have realized the trick was to start with the trial, seal off the courtroom––prohibiting anybody from leaving––and then interrogate all the spectators. This technique worked wonders for detective Charlie Chan. Dollars to donuts says the murderer would be in the courtroom. The concept of leaving town just never occurred to the rogues in Perry Mason stories. They always came back, like spawning salmon.

Perry Mason was one major reason I became a lawyer. I obviously did not do so for the money. And speaking of money the next fictional lawyer who is one of the most iconic attorneys I can think of is Atticus Finch from *To Kill a Mockingbird* fame. When I mention money, I am not suggesting at all that Atticus Finch was a greedy lawyer. On the contrary.

I had the pleasure of recently seeing the movie again. If you remember, the movie is a 1962 classic drama about a lawyer, Atticus Finch, played by Oscar award-winning Gregory Peck, who defends a black man charged with raping a white girl in a small southern town in the early 1930s. One scene impressed me very much. The accused, Atticus Finch's client, is transferred from the county jail to the unguarded town jail the night before his trial starts. When Atticus hears rumours that a lynch mob might try to expedite the course of justice, he brings along a chair, a tall reading lamp, and a good book and he parks himself in front of the town jail in order to guard his client the entire night from the anticipated mob, which ultimately arrives.

Although I first saw this movie before I ever considered going to law school, viewing it this time as a lawyer, this scene was very significant. I asked myself the question all other lawyers would immediately ask: Would a government Legal Aid program cover Atticus' full fee for all his efforts in this type of situation? I imagined for the purposes of this fantasy that the provisions of the Ontario Legal Aid Plan are at least as comprehensive as those of the state's Legal Aid Plan of the 1930s. A lawyer's account to Legal Aid might in part read as follows:

"July 11. To preparation for trial, including spending night in front of town jail guarding client from lynch mob, to addressing members of lynch mob and calming them down, to reassuring client, 11 p.m. to 7 a.m."

The main problem facing the lawyer is that the Legal Aid tariff allows a maximum amount of preparation time for trials and other procedural or substantive steps. If say the tariff allows eight hours pre-trial preparation time for the first day of a trial, then counsel has already consumed this allotted time for preparation. There is hope. He could get down on his knees and beg for additional alms by referring to the tariff schedules and asking for the discretionary increase. There are a number of schedules dealing with an increase request. The account would therefore continue something like this:

"Pursuant to Schedule 2, I would ask for an extension of the eight hours maximum in view of the following circumstances. I heard rumours that a lynch mob would be arriving at the town jail that night to visit my client. I also heard that local authorities were unwilling or unable to spend the night guarding my client. I thought it prudent to undertake the task myself. The result obtained was excellent as indeed the mob arrived ready to hang my client, but after some discourse, it left the scene in peace. The offence itself was serious, namely rape. There was an additional complexity. I had to spend the whole night sitting outside on a hard wooden chair. I think I deserve an additional $150."

Notwithstanding the schedule, the ultimate recovery could still be tempered by the provisions of the tariff requiring "pre-authorization" for greater time allowances in cases that fall into the complex-case categories. These provisions requiring clearance, which I'll call "Note X," look something like this:

"Where a solicitor can readily ascertain that services authorized by a certificate, in the specific circumstances of that case, are sufficiently unusual or unique that the maximum allowed by the tariff is clearly inadequate, he shall forth-with advise the area director and Legal Accounts Officer of the details of the case and an estimate of the time and services required in his opinion. Failure of a solicitor to do so will be a factor in the settlement of the solicitor's account."

Then again, diligent counsel would whip over by courier a letter to the Legal Accounts Officer with a copy to the area director, all in accordance with Note X.

"Dear Sir:

This case is very unusual. I don't think tariff maximum of eight hours for preparation for the first day of a rape trial will cover it all as I expect to spend several hours tonight alone in front of the Town Jail guarding my client. It's hard to say exactly how long I'll be there, but I think I'll need more than my allotted eight hours for preparation.

As for other details, I expect a lynch mob composed of 20 to 30 men, clad in overalls and straw hats and carrying shotguns and axe handles."

Now if counsel keeps Note X in mind, then after asking for a Note X increase, he stands a chance of getting his additional $150. Judging from experience, however, it's most unlikely that he will be reimbursed for the courier. I don't know if and how Atticus Finch got paid for going beyond the usual call of duty as a lawyer but his actions were commendable, an inspiration to us all.

And speaking of Finch, how about flinch? I talk of Sir Wilfred Robarts, the British barrister played by Charles Laughton in the Oscar-winning film,

Witness for the Prosecution. What caught my eye was Sir Wilfred's monocle test, which he performed on every potential client who came into his office. He would stare at them and question them while looking through his small glass monocle, which reflected light on their faces like an inquisitor's lamp. If the people being questioned flinched, then they were usually lying. Was the test accurate? At least Sir Wilfred thought it was. Maybe one day it will become a staple in legal proceedings. The court staff could hand out monocles to the jury members and they could perform the test themselves.

As their popularity increases, it would not be too long before retailers start selling them. I can see Costco getting on board. "Special this week, the truth monocle." Given Costco's usual packaging practices of selling in bulk, they likely would sell a package containing two monocles. Then again, this could be a problem as two monocles may not constitute a monocle; it might be considered one pair of regular glasses. You can get these anytime at their optical department. No doubt something to be ironed out. But as of today, this monocle test is still fiction. As are Perry Mason, Atticus Finch, and Sir Wilfred Robarts. But what giants these characters are!

Actually, there is another lawyer I have in mind who impressed me. I think of Sidney Carton, the barrister of Dickens's *A Tale of Two Cities* fame. And since we're talking about fiction, my mind has wandered off again and I have come up with lawyer Sydney Barton in *A Far, Far Better Tale*. This story appears at the end of this chapter. Actually, we are just about at the end so here it is, as promised.

A Far, Far Better Tale

It was the best of times, it was the worst of times, it was a time of wisdom, it was a time of foolishness, it was a time of similarity, it was a time of contrast. Edmonton Alberta was a strange place in the nineteen sixties. But this tale is about France in the late 1700s. It was a time of oppression. The nobility called all the shots, trampling on the peasants. Those were the 1780s; the twenty-first century had not yet arrived in France.

Dr. Monette was in the Bastille. He was a plastic surgeon and dermatologist sentenced to twenty years at hard labour for allegedly starting the great dandruff epidemic of the 1770s. The epidemic spared no one. All of France was flaking.

Now a word about the Bastille. It was like a jail. It was built to hold 350 prisoners, but in 1789 it held only 28; nobody wanted to go there. It was a veritable fortress, indestructible. It withstood even the great fire of London in 1666.

Meanwhile, back in England. Ahhh England. Sidney Barton was a prominent barrister, a champion of the underdog. He pleaded many of his cases for no fee; he did them on Legal Aid certificates. It was said that not one of his clients ever went to the guillotine.

Fifteen years ago, Sidney Barton was afflicted with boils on his scalp. This made wearing a wig in court very cumbersome. He would always have to start his trials by asking leave of the court pursuant to Rule 187 of the Rules of Court to dispense with the wearing of a wig. British medical doctors were baffled by the disease, unable to find a cure. The great dermatologist, Sir Geoffrey of Chester, said of Sidney Barton, "I wouldn't want him to marry my daughter." Sidney Barton visited Sir Geoffrey's office frequently and Sir Geoffrey would say to his assistant, "Is he gone yet?"

And how did Sidney Barton overcome this affliction? Dr. Monette of course. In the year 1777 Sidney was making one of his frequent visits to Paris to commit suicide. This time he intended to go through with it. He decided to jump into the icy Seine River. Suddenly he came across Dr. Monette who was relieving himself under the Pont Neuf. The good doctor shouted, "Non! Don't do eet."

Sidney decided not to jump into the water for now. Instead, he reached for his pistol but realized that he must have dropped it in the taxi on route to the Seine. Dr. Monette rushed up to Sidney Barton and introduced himself. The two chatted for a few minutes and they became immediate friends. Dr. Monette offered to treat Sidney at his clinic. After six weeks, voila, the boils were gone.

Upon Sidney's return to court, at the start of his first case, the presiding judge, Lord Levine, asked Sidney, "So, you're not asking for relief under Rule 187 today?" Meanwhile the situation in France deteriorated rapidly. Queen Marie Antoinette told the people of France to eat cake. They did. After six months the average Frenchman put on some ten kilos. Tooth decay was rampant.

One day Gavroche, a Paris sewer maintenance inspector, came down with an awful toothache after a steady diet of brioches and jam. He could take it no longer and he gathered a mob near Place de la Vendome. Within hours he and about 25,000 other disgruntled pastry eaters, many with dental problems, stormed the Bastille and the French Revolution was on.

The revolutionaries were ruthless. They grabbed the warden of the Bastille and stuffed buttered croissants into each of his ears. The prison guards were pelted with cinnamon buns. The mob proceeded to release the prisoners of the Bastille. When Gavroche himself came across Dr. Monette and heard that he was a doctor he was ecstatic. Suddenly he gave the doctor a good whack across the face; he was disappointed that the doctor did not turn out to be a dentist!

The Revolution continued. The nobility were harassed wherever they travelled, especially on the roads. The police hid behind billboards along all roads and whenever a big shot or his associate drove by, they would stop him and give him a traffic summons. The blue bloods would be charged with the usual traffic offences, including speeding, careless driving, and making love in a carriage parked in the vicinity of Notre Dame Cathedral in Paris.

At times the police would outdo themselves. One Maurice de la Filet, a cousin of Louis XVI, was charged with the latter offence and he was caught doing it in Marseilles. He was found guilty and fined 1,000 francs plus 25,000 francs for towing. The traffic courts were bursting at the seams with aristocratic traffic charges. Pretty soon the justice system broke down and trials became a mockery. Mobs would jam the body of the court and cheer and jeer as if the proceedings were a sporting event. The mob was usually taunted by that vixen Madame Lefarge, a proletarian. She and her husband, Mario, had once owned a local tavern and house of pleasure.

She had good reason to hate the nobility. One night her house, or "la maison," as it was called, was frequented by the gluttonous Baron de Knack. The Baron fell asleep in one of the rooms but in his excitement, he forgot to extinguish his cigar. Naturally, the whole place burned to the ground. When Madame Lafarge tried to make a claim against her insurance, she was denied coverage. The insurance company, Royale Assurance, was owned by King Louis XVI. The claims adjuster pointed out a specific exemption clause in the insurance policy that read, "No insurance paid for a fire caused by spontaneous combustion." The insurance company insisted that the Baron just suddenly ignited.

Madame Lafarge was beside herself. She could not afford the exorbitant fees lawyers usually charge in order to sue that wealthy, monstrous, callous, and heartless insurance company, and so she let it go after that. She decided to take up knitting instead. She also started hating lawyers at that time, even people who looked like lawyers.

Back in the courtrooms the verdict in each case was obvious. The writing was on the wall. One day Marquis St. Zotique, brother-in-law of His Majesty, was convicted after a five-minute trial of speeding in a school zone and the judge had not yet even entered the court room! When the Marquis protested, he was also held responsible for the writing on the wall and fined another 500 francs.

Then one day it happened. Dr. Monette, while driving his carriage in a suburb of Paris, was stopped by the police and charged with tailgating another carriage.

"But monsieur la police," he protested, "there is no carriage in sight in front of me."

"But of course not Monsieur le Docteur," replied monsieur la police, "You chased heem away."

It may be useful at this point to advise that the doctor was Baron de Knack's personal dermatologist and the policeman was none other than Monsieur Lafarge. After la maison was lost, he eventually joined the police morality squad.

Dr. Monette was summoned to court to face trial on the charge. He knew what a conviction would mean. He would be fined 250 francs and then he would be forced to undergo the tortuous driver-improvement course. He knew that at the course the likes of Madame Lefarge would gather to laugh at him while he would be made to practise his driving skills in a simulation vehicle, namely, a team of wooden horses. The mob would laugh while he would have to pull at the reins and shout: "Yip, yip, voila, yip, yip voila. Whoa."

Dr. Monette was tried, convicted, sentenced, and remanded in custody. Sidney Barton heard about the doctor's plight. He knew how this degrading experience would upset the doctor and accordingly he decided to act. He had a plan. The doctor was seventy-five years old and Sidney was forty-seven. The doctor was tall and skinny and Sidney was short and stout. The doctor also had acne. Sidney's plan was to travel to Paris, sneak into the jail, and switch places with Dr. Monette. Foolproof, *oui*?

The next day Sidney Barton secretly arrived in Paris. In a couple of hours, the doctor was to be given "the horse," as it was called. Sidney arrived at the jail and convinced the guard, Jacques, that he was Dr. Monette's lawyer. Unfortunately, Jacques delayed Sidney for over an hour asking for advice about his own matrimonial problems. Sidney did not know the first thing about French law but he did what any first-year law student would do; he proceeded to give legal advice. At the conclusion, Jacques asked, "What is adultery?"

Sidney Barton entered the cell of Dr. Monette together with his assistant Ehrlick. Ehrlick was a weightlifter from Liverpool. The plan was to knock Dr. Monette out with a chloroform-soaked handkerchief, have Sidney Barton and the doctor exchange clothing and have Ehrlick remove the doctor from the jail. All did not go as planned. The doctor momentarily turned around and Ehrlick clubbed him on the head with his fists. It seems that Sidney forgot his chloroform bottle in the taxi en route to the jail. An old habit.

The clothing switch was made and Ehrlick carried the doctor out of the jail. As they passed the guards, one of them asked, "Who is the guy with the acne?" Jacques replied, "That's my lawyer. By the way what is adultery?"

Back at the cell, Sidney Barton was proud of himself. At last he could repay the debt owed to his dear friend Dr. Monette. A special team of guards came to pick up Sidney Barton and he was taken by carriage to Place de la Bastille. He thought to himself, "It is a far, far better thing I do now than I have ever done before."

Dr. Monette was well on his way to England by now, where he would wake up soon with a big headache. Sidney Barton was strapped to the horse. The test was about to start when Madame Lefarge suddenly shouted, "This is not Dr. Monette, he looks like a lawyer. He must be a lawyer."

"And what of it madame," said Sidney Barton.

"You thought it was a far, far better thing you did now, didn't you?" shouted the madame. "Proceed with the test anyway." The guards put Sidney Barton through the test. The mob laughed and cheered as Sidney shouted at the wooden horses. "Yip, yip, voila. Yip, yip, voila. Whoa." He passed the test with a mark of ninety-four, better than most French drivers.

He was subsequently charged with impersonating a plastic surgeon and dermatologist and his penalty was banishment from France. He was ordered to be put on a ferry boat, without food or water, bound for Dover. The captain of the boat was told to navigate the thirty or so kilometres very, very slowly so that it would hurt. As the boat left the harbour at Calais, a gentleman ran out on the dock and tossed a pistol and a bottle at Sidney

Barton. "This must be yours," he shouted. It was a taxi driver who had found Sidney's pistol and a bottle of chloroform.

Don't we all need more Sydney Bartons. Mais oui!

These legal beagles are of course associated with a courtroom. But is the courtroom the only forum for resolution of legal disputes? What about alternate dispute resolution, especially in civil litigation?

CHAPTER TWENTY-NINE

Alternative Dispute Resolution: Fireside Chat on How to Deal With the Fires

"Discourage litigation. Persuade your neighbors to compromise whenever you can. … As a peacemaker the lawyer has superior opportunity of being a good man. There will still be business enough."
~ Abraham Lincoln

Sounds good to me. En garde! Shall we mediate? Why? Mediation was
certainly unheard of when I went to law school. The game plan was
learning the law to educate you to maneuver through the court system to
enable you to win your case.

I recall studying *Donoghue v. Stevenson*, that snail in the ginger beer
House of Lords landmark negligence decision. I don't recall the torts professor saying anything about whether the parties ever tried to resolve the
action through mediation. Perhaps these days the prof might say, "What
can we learn from this case? If you say negligence, you're wrong. The
real lesson is that a good mediator could have gotten this case settled out
of court."

Then again it would not have been too helpful had the case resolved at a mediation. How would the law reports read? "*Donoghue v. Stevenson* negligence case resolved; settlement terms confidential."

I wonder what the history of mediation is. There was certainly no shortage of disputes and wars throughout. Empires bent on conquest from Alexander the Great to Hannibal to Julius Caesar came and went. Nowhere in my research did I come across anything like Roman legions gathering at the border with Gaul, waiting for go-ahead to attack and plunder should mediation scheduled for Thursday fail.

You might say King Solomon was a mediator when he intervened to resolve that dispute between those two women who claimed to be the mother of that baby. Each lady gave birth, one's died and they both claimed the live one was hers. The wise king offered to cut the baby in two and give each party half. The rogue mom of course agreed, making it obvious to the king who the real mom was not. (Good thing it was obvious as this case could have been a real mess.)

When I started practising in the 1970s, litigation was litigation. You issued a claim, went on to examinations for discovery, and your case culminated in a trial. Winner take all.

Eventually, alternative dispute resolution started to germinate in my jurisdiction with the advent of the judicial pre-trial. We would attend with our clients and have a resolution meeting with a judge for about an hour. The lawyers were required to file a *short* couple-of-pages summary to give the judge an idea about the case. The problem for many lawyers was the operative word "pages." Merriam-Webster's dictionary defines short as "having little length." No doubt to many lawyers Tolstoy's epic *War and Peace* would fall into this word-size category.

Very often the judge, after listening to some wrangling between the lawyers, would shrug his or her shoulders and say something like, "If this case goes to trial, someone will get their ass kicked. Though often helpful, an hour or so was not enough to bring about the desired settlement.

Mediation started to become popular here in the 1980s. A neutral person properly informed sits down for a few hours with parties willing to settle. And for mediation to work it helps if you have a competent mediator. I have noticed a few styles of mediators:

The Courier

This person simply virtually delivers offers and counter offers to the parties sitting in their respective breakout rooms. The drill looks like this:

Mediator: They want $1 million dollars. What do you say?

Defendant lawyer: No way. We'll pay $20,000.

Mediator: OK. I'll deliver your counter to them.

They offer few suggestions for resolution. Given what they are paid, it might be just as effective and certainly cheaper to use an agent from U.P.S.

Mediator (in plaintiff's room): They're offering $20,000.

Plaintiff lawyer: Tell them we'll take $850,000.

Mediator: OK. Will do.

Plaintiff's lawyer (thinking): I'm surprised this guy isn't wearing that brown uniform.

The Former Judge

Though knowledgeable, many former judges still think like judges. Firstly, often they have not left their egos back in the courtroom. When they walk into the mediation room they have that air about them as if they almost expect some clerk to bellow, "Oyez, oyez, oyez. All rise." They will remind you they were judges for twenty years and they know what's best for the parties. They'll remind the parties of the perils of litigation, saying something like, "If this case goes to trial, someone will get their ass kicked."

The Pusher

This mediator is the opposite of the courier. He or she is gung-ho to get this case resolved. Sometimes too gung-ho:

Mediator: They want $1 million dollars. What do you say?

Defendant Lawyer: No way. We'll pay $20,000.

Mediator (in defendant's room): The plaintiff comes across as sympathetic. You do know a jury listening to him could hit you for millions? This case is worth settling today.

Mediator (in plaintiff's room): They're offering $20,000. As you know, juries are unpredictable. And a bird in the hand is …

At least this mediator works hard, fervently wanting the case to settle.

One problem with the mediation culture is that many lawyers lose the opportunity to acquire trial skills. Sure, given the vagaries of litigation, a just settlement is nothing to sneeze at. On the other hand, I know of many younger lawyers in practice for several years who have never or rarely conducted a trial, jury, or even bench. Can they handle a trial? Should lawyers lament the dwindling opportunities of trial experience?

King Solomon was wise. I think of another wise man, Albert Einstein, who reputedly said, "A ship is always safe at shore, but that is not what it's built for." As we will recall, Einstein also said, "Intellectuals solve problems. Geniuses prevent them."

What else can I say about mediation? I agree with Einstein, whatever he says. And I certainly agree with Lincoln. I will add that many mediators in addition to retired judges are also retired lawyers. Which gets me to retirement. What else do retired lawyers do now? And what does Einstein have to say about aging?

CHAPTER THIRTY

What Happens to Retired Lawyers? Just Deserts

"I have reached an age when if someone tells
me to wear socks, I don't have to."
~ Albert Einstein

As my hair started turning salt and peppery, the most common question I faced was, "Are you retired yet?" The second most common was, "When do you plan to retire?"

Lawyers retire and then what? What changes? Well, my hair is now more salty than peppery, and I stopped my litigation practice several years ago. Does retirement take the lawyer out of the lawyer?

My first notable change was the abated urge to meticulously read everything I would have to sign. When I rented a car, I'd be the one holding up the line as I asked the clerk questions, such as, "What do you mean in point 48 by 'the customer is responsible for'...?" This urge has diminished. Were the document to read, "Sign on the line above where it says, Dr. Faustus," I'd consider it.

I also find my patience has diminished. While in practice I typically spent hours parsing lengthy agreements. Now I am uncomfortable dealing with even the simplest of forms. I received a Canada census form recently and it troubled me to complete it even though it was their "short form" version. I needed a break after confirming the pre-populated information of my name, age, and address. I felt like adding, "Hey, don't bug me. I'm retired."

Bookkeeping is also an issue. Whereas I routinely was able to carry in my head a divorcing client's detailed financial status (as well as their spouse's), these days review of my own simple checking bank account annoys me. Rather than review it monthly, I often tell myself, "It's a bank; it must be OK."

Then again, I played Monopoly with my granddaughter, and I drew the "Chance" card, reading, "Bank error in your favour. Collect $200." This troubled me. After the game, I rushed to check my bank statement. But I still didn't like doing it. I thought of life after death and just hoped that wherever I end up, they don't turn me into a forensic accountant. Which leads me to civility.

I can proudly say that I never resorted to personal or *ad hominem* attacks. (That's a Latin phrase – sorry.) Well, maybe as Gilbert and Sullivan's Captain Corcoran said in *HMS Pinafore*, "Hardly ever."

I note though tempted, I have been successful post-retirement in maintaining this trait. I checked in for a flight once and though we had fee-free luggage rewards status, the clerk said the "system" did not note this information and he demanded $60. He insisted I pay now and notify customer service later. I was livid. I was about to tell him where he can go. (I was thinking about that place I feared they may turn me into a forensic accountant.) But after decades of exercising restraint to remain civil, while signing the credit card authorization I just said, "Thank you, sir. Unfortunately, on this transaction I don't see an option to leave a tip."

Continuing legal education is another area of change. So long mandatory Continuing Legal Education (CLE) annual hours. Now I can just learn what I want when I want to. I took one class on insurance changes just for fun. One speaker was over the top dull, incongruent, and incomprehensible. He may as well have spoken in Middle Phoenician. In the past I would have hit the dialogue box and I would likely have said something like, "Sir, can you please explain that point again about 'no coverage'? It sounds crystal clear, but I must be missing something." Now I just say to myself, "Hey, who cares. I don't have to know this stuff anymore. I'm retired."

People ask about how I spend my days. The better question is how I used to spend them. I used to stress come Sunday evenings, knowing Monday I had to jump into the lion's den, the fire pit, or at times the ten-ring circus. I called the feeling the "Monday-morning blues." Eventually I started getting the Monday-morning blues earlier on Sunday, and then progressively even earlier. Friday morning would arrive, and I'd feel good initially. Then I'd ruminate, "Hey, Monday is only seventy-two hours away." I soon developed a Friday midday blues syndrome.

Approaching age seventy is not a good time to be agitated. I longed for the opportunity to be able to just do little, simple things, like loaf. Actually, though loafing is great, my lifelong passion was writing humour full time. As I was nearing age seventy, I thought about that adage, the best time to plant an oak tree is twenty years ago. The second-best time is today.

Was age an issue? I noted that Winston Churchill became PM, hitting the big time, at age sixty-six. And Colonel Harland Sanders sold his first franchise while in his sixties. Even Stalin reached his prime as a senior. I, of course, had a different product to offer than Churchill, and certainly different than Stalin. And at least my name wasn't Harland.

I now follow my passion, having recently launched my third book, *Boomers, Zoomers and Other Oomers: A Boomer-biased Irreverent Perspective on Aging*. It may be of interest to anyone who's aged since starting to read this story. A fun read any day of the week. (Plug done.)

Now getting up on Monday morning is a nonissue. Sometimes I forget what day it is. I just know it ends with the suffix "day." That's all I must know. Hey, I'm retired. Einstein had it right. I am not talking about his theory of relativity. As I write these words, I have chosen not to wear socks.

CHAPTER THIRTY-ONE

Humour in the Practice
of Law—Seriously?

"When humor goes, there goes civilization."
~ Erma Bombeck

Are you sometimes overstressed going about your daily business, or if a lawyer, practising law? Is your sense of humour dormant or even worse, muzzled? Of course not, but if it is ...

Actually, lawyers are not generally regarded as the instruments of jest. There is a general reticence in the profession to lighten up. Let me share ten tips and thoughts on how and why I used humour successfully while in practice. And you need not be a lawyer to benefit from these suggestions.

1. Health benefits
Humour and laughter can relieve stress and enhance health, lowering blood pressure, and by releasing endorphins, ease pain. Good so far?

2. Rapport
I made it a point on commencing a case to telephone opposing counsel, ensuring a giggle or two followed quickly. In a nasty divorce matter, I told

the lawyer his letter to my client sounded like it was penned by Captain Bligh. He chuckled. The ice was broken and he soon conceded that his client was not pushing spousal support and would settle for a reasonable property adjustment. We averted a mutiny on the Bounty. So why the reluctance to use it?

3. Humour is not serious

I once had a pre-trial meeting with a Crown attorney (aka District Attorney south of the Canadian border) regarding a repeater shoplifter. A jail term was imminent. After some banter we came to a deal for a fine. The Crown wrote in his brief, "A fine is fine." He then said, "No, this looks like I'm making light of the matter." He revised it to "A fine is OK." Now that's serious!

Humour is anything but unserious. Research has shown that many Fortune 500 businesses routinely hire consultants to bring some fun into the lives of their companies' operations. Herb Kelleher, former CEO of Southwest Airlines, credited a large part of the company's 25-year consecutive profit success to his irreverent management style.

He said, "We should take our jobs seriously but never ourselves." Kelleher propounded that there is a direct relationship between having fun on the job and productivity. He would sometimes show up to work dressed as Elvis. Or occasionally personally deliver a passenger's lost luggage. Kelleher would say, "We should take our jobs seriously, but never ourselves." Herb K., incidentally, received a law degree at New York University. Seriously!

Hey, Ukraine's president, Volodymyr Zelensky, in better times was actually a comedian. And did you know he also has a law degree? Seriously!

Note that Abraham Lincoln maintained his sense of humour even in the midst of a great war (which was rather serious).

Lincoln would start a war cabinet meeting during the early part of the Civil War by reading passages from a humourist author. His cabinet remained gloomy, wondering how the president can turn to humour given the seriousness of the meeting. Lincoln did not waiver or apologize. He said, "Gentlemen, why don't you laugh? With the fearful strain that is upon me night and day, if I did not laugh I should die, and you need this medicine as much as I do."

Noted psychiatrist Viktor Frankl, Holocaust survivor and author of bestseller *Man's Search for Meaning*, encouraged concentration-camp inmates to use humour whenever possible, noting individuals were able to employ humour to give them even a short respite from the horrors of the camps, thereby increasing their chances of survival.

Were these notable people making light of wars and ordeals? Or were they using humour to ease stress? Humour is known to do just that as well as enhance rapport and team bonding and spark creativity. We are not talking about jokes per se, but rather how one views a situation. And how does the public perceive lawyers? I tell people that I write humour and a common response is, "A humorous lawyer? That's an oxymoron." Relish that image?

4. You need to be Seinfeld (not that there's any ...)

What generates humour? Anything not perfect. In one word: *Imperfecshun*. And since nothing is perfect, everything can be viewed through a lens of humour, from weather to traffic to judges. Even perfection is humorous. Please forgive me for repeating what that sage Yogi Berra said, "If the world were perfect, it wouldn't be. (After all to forgive is divine. But still not perfect). Yo Yogi.

5. Humour is per se offensive?

In today's climate, people are afraid their humorous comments may cause trouble. What to do? Ask if your goal is to promote goodwill or to insult or amuse haphazardly. Set your compass to common sense.

When a colleague would not return my communications, instead of sending a nasty message, I would often e-mail, saying: "I can think of only three reasons why you're ignoring me:

i. You're extremely busy,

ii. You're paying me back for ignoring you, or

iii. You discovered it was I who deflated the tires of your new BMW.

I always got a quick response, often with an apology. And amazingly, humour begets humour. One colleague responded noting reason number three. (Little did he know ...)

I'd like to share some of my humour tricks of the trade.

6. Pictures, puppets, and posters, oh my!

• I had a wall corkboard with *Far Side* cartoons. I also had a poster of a handsome beagle bearing the caption, "Everything I need to know in life I learned from my dog."

• My desk sported a puppet of cartoon character Foghorn Leghorn, the southern gentleman rooster. You squeezed his belly and he blurted out, "Ah say, go away son. You bother me."

• I invited distressed clients to squeeze old Foghorn. They would giggle and feel better, until I told them "Laugh, laugh. You're paying me $X per hour. Then I'd say, "Only kidding; I should pay you for making me laugh."

I never lost a client for importing humour. Using humour says that their lawyer is also human.

7. Borrow from the wise; Churchill said ...

Another useful method for generating humour is reading from a cute news story or using a quote. You will get all the credit for the chuckles.

On an estate issue, I would quote French humourist, Rabelais, who said his Will reads, "I have little. I owe much. The rest I leave to the poor."

Borrow some wisdom from notables such as Sir Winston Churchill. My favourite Churchillian quote, in speaking of a rival is, "That man has all of the virtues I despise and none of the vices I admire." Doesn't this beat using nasty or vile lingo?

8. Target yourself

Humour comes easier when you are the target. For sure, you will have little resistance. A successful colleague of mine when presented with a lowball offer, rather than assailing the offeror would often respond, "Hey, when I last looked at my driver's licence, it said Sydney Cooper, not Homer Simpson."

We all have a sense of humour. As Stephen Leacock said, "The world's humour, in its best and greatest sense is perhaps the highest product of our civilization."

9. But ...

Humour is not a panacea for all the world's problems. John Cleese of Monty Python fame notes, "When you charge the enemy machine-gun post, don't waste energy trying to see the funny side of it." In short, use humour appropriately.

I know. That's only nine tips. Hey, I'm not perfect.

CHAPTER THIRTY-TWO

We Respectfully Conclude

"Always do right. This will gratify some people and astonish the rest."
~ Mark Twain

B ack in my high school and university days I was an avid tournament chess player. I amassed a fine collection of chess books that I came across recently. My favourite was a book titled *How Not to Play Chess*. It resonated with me as it got me thinking laterally, outside the box so to speak (or rather in this case outside the squares).

Focusing my sights on the legal universe, I muse about not how people should think about lawyers and the legal system but rather how they should not think about them (and it).

Looking at the markers I mentioned in Chapter 2, "Why Everybody Loves Lawyers—Sort Of)," let me run through a few of these alleged or so-called blemishes attributed to the profession, from this perspective:

Dollars
Yes Virginia, lawyers do generally want to get paid for their services. But do lawyers really earn outrageous incomes? The Province of Ontario's Legal Aid Plan is designed to help the indigent who cannot afford a lawyer to

represent them in serious matters. The plan has a fee tariff that roughly ranges from about $120ish to about $180ish per hour, depending on the experience of the lawyer and complexity of the case. The higher end would be paid to an experienced lawyer for handling a murder case for example. So were that hypothetical lawyer to spend 8 hours a day on that case, where if convicted his client goes to jail for life, this works out to $1,440/day or $7,200/week.

Assuming the lawyer does take some time off and works say 48 weeks per year, the total gross income would be about $345,600/year. I did say gross. Overhead can easily eat up 40–50% of that amount, and even taking the lower end, that leaves the lawyer with about $207k per year (before taxes, eh!).

Remember those athletes earning millions per year don't have to worry about overhead. I doubt the Maple Leafs ace player Austin Mathews sits down with a sharp pencil too often muttering comments such as, "More problems with the ice surface. I'll have to go to the bank and get a loan for a new Zamboni."

Of course, there are the civil cases, such as matrimonial/family cases where spouses do not get along and where they are not eligible for legal aid and where each must pay big bucks to hire legal representation. These parties have options. Most often where they are reasonable and non-combative, they can come to a peaceful resolution quickly, with the help of the lawyers. The lawyers do not create the war. I did say reasonable and non-combative. As Charles Dickens said, "If there were no bad people, there would be no good lawyers."

However, I will say that most lawyers who handle family-law matters will agree that given the emotional barometer, this area is the most stressful one. We face personal threats, assaults, communications at many odd hours from apprehensive clients, child kidnappings or worse, and certainly more emergency situations, often requiring you to drop what you're doing and run to court for some type of remedy.

I think back to a law student, Sam, who once worked for me. We spent months on a flagship highly charged case involving custody and visitation rights to children, allegations of violence, breaches of court orders, restraining orders, urgent court attendances, etc. At the end of his work term, I wondered whether he would want to handle family-law cases one day once called to the Bar, and I asked him what he had learned from all of this. He replied, "I learned never to get married." At least the experience did not tarnish his humour.

The better question is, are the clients protected from possible gouging? As mentioned earlier, unlike most other callings I can think of, our system does provide for a procedure to assess a lawyer's account. This procedure keeps the lawyer's bills honest. As well Ontario does have a well-established contingency fee system. As many lawyers' ads read, "You don't pay if we do not collect." True it may not apply to family-law matters. But don't shoot the lawyers.

As for contingency arrangements I will say my worst experience was working on an injury case for seven years, where the client was hurt by some falling merchandise at a large box store. Unfortunately, the jury did not buy most of it and my fee at the end of it all was zero. (When you're all finished playing your fiddles and going "ahhhh," I'll continue.) *Ergo* no, let's not first kill the lawyers. (*Ergo* is Latin. Please disregard if you wish.)

Honesty and Transparency

No, don't trust me. But most lawyers are indeed honest. Our Rules of Professional Conduct ethics is replete with admonitions along the lines of don't do anything to bring the legal profession into disrepute, or don't engage in conduct unbecoming of a lawyer. Section **2.1-1** of the Rules reads: "A lawyer has a duty to carry on the practice of law and discharge all responsibilities to clients, tribunals, the public, and other members of the profession honourably and with integrity."

OK, but do we all heed these rules? I have already noted what Yogi Berra would say. My point is honesty and integrity are embedded in the ethos or ideology of the profession. While most other callings no doubt expect their practitioners to be honest, and most of them likely are, I doubt they are governed by the rules lawyers are expected to follow, rules that rival in stringency and relevance of the Ten Commandments. In short, at least we are expected to be honest.

Let's not overlook this *credo* (oops, Latin again. Let's call it "tenet").

Ambulance Chasers

Right again, a law practice is a business. And many lawyers do advertise as do other businesses. We all know who these outfits are, but after a few minutes of watching some sporting or other program on television, we will all get reminded to drink Coca Cola, eat at McDonald's, or bring our money to the TD Bank. I have never heard anybody accuse these companies of being quench, hunger, or money chasers respectively. Does it not really get down to the advertisements being in good taste?

I previously mentioned that local firm that posts its ads on the walls over urinals. Not a place to tout legal services. I will admit that while doing my business at a public urinal, I never found myself looking ahead and being stared in the face by a Big Mac.

Ambulance chasers? Most importantly the majority of lawyers don't even advertise—or for that matter deal with accident matters.

Duration of Cases

What did Einstein say about the relatively of time? There is a quote apparently attributed to this genius that goes, "When you sit with a nice girl for two hours, you think it's only a minute, but when you sit on a hot stove for a minute, you think it's two hours. That's relativity."

I cannot think of other callings that can take as long to resolve as some legal cases do. I recently went to the supermarket to buy a fresh barbecued chicken and the clerk told me they are still cooking and they wouldn't be ready for another half hour. The half hour felt like an eternity. I was tempted to say to the clerk, "Hey, are you nuts? We're starving." I then thought about that Einstein quote and relaxed. Putting a positive spin on it, unlike those chickens, at least I did not have to be near that hot stove.

Then again, comparing a legal action to other professions such as medicine, even brain surgery takes only a few hours. Similarly dental procedures generally take less than an hour or so, although they sometimes feel like an eternity.

What can we do to expedite matters? Limit discovery procedures? Shrink the availability of trials by jury? This one I have no problem with. Allowing a group of lay people without any legal knowledge to make decisions on major financial or human-liberty matters does not sit well with me. Getting back to that brain surgery, I shudder to think what would happen in the O.R. if you would have twelve people sitting nearby and the surgeon has to ask them, "I'm ready to cut. Is this area of the skull a good place to start?"

Also, speaking of delays, is there a deficiency of judges? I don't know. I actually once applied to become a judge, but I was never accepted. If the justice system was hurting as a result of not having enough judges, too bad. They missed their opportunity.

And of course, it does not help that lawyers are often accused of being windbags. I once presented a client with a Will I drafted. The client saw the words "give, devise, and bequeath" and asked me, "Why can't we just say 'I give?' I'm sure my kids will be happy." I could not give him a satisfactory answer. At least I got the Will drafted and ready by Friday.

When I think of duration until resolution, for some reasons I think about how long it took to complete the construction of these European cathedrals such as the Cologne Cathedral in Germany. It was started in 1248 and completed in 1880. Yeah, wow!

I suppose on that fateful day in 1248, a few important church and city officials gathered on the site and made speeches. The archbishop, probably optimistically, said something like, "Until now we have had to pray in that little kirche on Ludvig Strasse, which could barely accommodate 150 worshipers. Once we finish this cathedral, we will be able to accommodate one thousand people. I look forward to celebrating mass with all of you in our beautiful Dom of Köln very soon." Right, Archbishop. And I hope to see the Toronto Maple Leafs win the Stanley Cup this century.

The mayor, or should I say "bürgermeister," was probably equally optimistic. I can just visualize him standing amongst the dignitaries, holding a large spade, and digging the first load of earth. Then he gets on the platform and announces proudly, "This is just the beginning." How right he would have been. Sort of like my maple tree. And no, the legal system is not that sluggish.

I doubt litigation cases will resolve much quicker through the courts. Then again maybe time is all relative? I doubt anybody ever tarred and feathered the contractors working on that Cologne Cathedral. So don't shoot all the lawyers.

And so, where is the legal system heading these days? Being a technophobe, I wonder about artificial intelligence, aka AI. In four words, I don't like it. It's definitely not A-1. Like I have confessed earlier, I am a technophobe. As I said initially, I started my litigation practice in 1974 B.C. (before computers). I experienced typewriters, carbon paper, and live people answering the telephones. (Hopefully, by now you millennials know what live people are.)

My experiences as a technophobe on steroids qualifies me sufficiently to comment on the subject of AI. I don't even like Google. I gather artificial intelligence is intelligence demonstrated by computers. I got this information from a trusted source, Google. This brings back thoughts to that 1960s film *2001: A Space Odyssey* where that computer HAL aboard a spaceship felt threatened by the humans and became quite aggressive. I guess it was intelligent enough to concern itself with self-preservation.

I also think about the Luddites, that group of English workers in the early 1800s who went around destroying machinery as they believed this equipment was threatening their jobs. I can somewhat empathize with the

Luddites, though fortunately I never felt the urge to invade any law offices and unplug their computers. And given all the wiring, I probably would not even know how to achieve this task.

AI is scary. Even Elon Musk has concerns about AI, noting that one of the biggest risks to the future of civilization is AI. I rest my case. Given this potential threat to civilization I am now thinking twice about buying a Tesla.

I find human contact is waning. For example, we telephone a bank with a query such as why the details of my bank account disappeared, and we are directed to go online where most of our questions can be answered. Right. And then you see that message online where you are supposed to prove that you are not a robot. Up pops that grid of about a dozen squares and you must tick off, say, all pictures showing a bus. I recently missed on that one as I counted one square that had only a bus driver in it. Maybe he was not even on the bus as the bus was being operated by a robot. Who knows?

Given that a robot probably is behind this harassing quiz, why does it care if you are a robot too? After all, if you are a robot, aren't you on his team? Robotic envy? How might AI permeate a litigation practice? What do I see in my crystal ball? Trials of course will be radically different with AI. The jurors will all be robots. This will speed up jury selection. The court registrar draws a card out of a drum and a robot stands up citing its name and occupation and lawyers can accept or challenge: "Zarkon 768 – fish packer at Costco."

Personally, I was always easy with jury selection, though I would likely challenge any robot with a face like a Picasso painting. I find I am sometimes untrustful about anybody with one ear on his chin, no mouth, and three noses. And the judge would not have to send this jury out for a *voir dire* while the lawyers argue over admissibility of evidence. The judge would just say to the jury, "Pay no attention to these lawyers now. They're just blabbing." The jury would likely respond in unison: "We obey." (During this hiatus, that Costco robot might just offer the visitors in the body of the court some samples of chopped herring.)

My concern is that juries might resort to technical shortcuts to arrive at a verdict. I can see them retiring to the jury room and the foreperson bellows out, "Hey Siri. Is the guy guilty or not guilty?" Which brings me back to the judge. Why not? After all, robots are putting together cars, performing surgery, and beating grandmasters in chess. Do we see the future trials adjudicated by robot judges? "Oyez, oyez, oyez, all rise for the judge, Justice SOL.83." And to keep pace with reality, some judges would have to be created nasty.

I did mention that judge who insisted male lawyers appearing before him wore black or gray pants, chewing out a poor lawyer unwittingly and daringly wearing brown pants and saying, "Counsel, I can't hear you." We may not be far from the day when a robot judge says to a lawyer, "Error, error. Please remove those red suspenders." I suppose the lawyers' gossip chatter about judges would be similar to the way it is now, with some twists.

"How's Justice X-311?"

"He's a hanging judge. But fortunately, my last appearance before him resulted in a mistrial. His battery ran out."

With A1 such as ChatGPT I also see potential confidentiality problems. Is it possible the robot could turn against the lawyer and use extortion? "Hey insurer, I know you are prepared to offer $1 million to settle this action. What's it worth to you for me not to divulge this information to the plaintiff's lawyer?" And we already see tech glitches happening. One ChatGPT recently listed as the third most visited sight in Ottawa, the Ottawa Food Bank. What else can go wrong in Ottawa?

But then of course there is no problem as you always have the availability, comfort, and ease of tech support. Just go online. Or hit some chat box. Or ask your personal robot.

So how do I feel about having spent decades as a practising lawyer? Charles Dickens comes to mind (once again) where he says, "It was the best of times, it was the worst of times, it was the spring of hope, it was the winter of despair, things were great, things were lousy." OK, Dickens didn't quite say that latter couplet. But isn't that the way it is for most of us? It helped greatly that I worked in a small firm; I was a sole practitioner. I always strove to do the right thing. I promptly returned messages, I always treated people with respect, and I never lost my cool. OK, hey, as Captain Corcoran of *H.M.S. Pinafore* might say, "hardly ever."

The motto of the Law Society of Ontario is "Let right prevail." But does it always prevail? Is right the same as justice? I think back to a matter where I represented a client in a forgery charge that with the help of a handwriting expert we were confident we could win. The Crown Attorney offered us a good deal, no jail time on a guilty plea. My client refused and I told the Crown he wanted justice. The case crashed and the client got convicted. Given some extenuating circumstances I asked for compassion in sentencing. The Crown responded, "Too bad. Plead guilty if you want compassion. Plead not guilty if you want justice." The client went to jail.

I guess we got justice. And presumably right. They never told us about these moments in law school. And I certainly worked hard on this case. I did not think I cheated on my "mistress."

I would say throughout my time in practice, in my respectful view, most of my clients were in the right. Most. Naturally. And yet my success rate was nowhere near 100%. But is not our job to uphold the principles of fairness and justice, acting civilly and with common sense, doing our best to try to get it right? I would like to think most of us entered this noble profession as we possess a preponderance of justice molecules in our DNA. And just maybe these molecules get stimulated early on by one experience or another, such as a fictional lawyer, or a down-to-earth parent with common sense, or that experience I had with those kindergarten bullies. I doubt those schoolyard bullies ever became lawyers. Or given their disposition, firefighters.

All in all, our profession is a dignified though not perfect one. I have never wavered from this view. I was happy and proud to make a few positive justice ripples on the universe and to put some smiles on people's faces. And I doubt I would have considered being anything else, such as a doctor, a professional athlete, or, though tempting, an Oscar Mayer frankfurter.